To Barb——
Wu

To the memory of Maggie Kuzwayo

Discipline
A Positive Guide for Parents

Martin Herbert

Basil Blackwell

Copyright © Martin Herbert 1989

First published 1989

Basil Blackwell Ltd
108 Cowley Road, Oxford, OX4 1JF, UK

Basil Blackwell Inc.
432 Park Avenue South, Suite 1503
New York, NY 10016, USA

All rights reserved. Except for the quotation of short passages for the purposes of criticism and review, no part of this publication may be reproduced, stored in a retrieval system, or transmitted, in any form or by any means, electronic, mechanical, photocopying, recording or otherwise, without the prior permission of the publisher.

Except in the United States of America, this book is sold subject to the condition that it shall not, by way of trade or otherwise, be lent, re-sold, hired out, or otherwise circulated without the publisher's prior consent in any form of binding or cover other than that in which it is published and without a similar condition including this condition being imposed on the subsequent purchaser.

British Library Cataloguing in Publication Data

A CIP catalogue record for this book is
available from the British Library

Library of Congress Cataloging in Publication Data

Herbert, Martin.
Discipline: a positive guide for parents/
by Martin Herbert.
    p.   cm.
Bibliography: p.
Includes index.
ISBN 0–631–16875–3
1. Discipline of children.   I. Title.
HQ770.4.H47   1989
649′64–dc19   88–27004

Typeset in 11 on 12½pt Stempel Garamond by
Ponting–Green Publishing Services, London
Printed in Great Britain by Billing & Sons Ltd, Worcester

Contents

List of guidelines   viii
Preface: Discipline without tears   x

1 Why discipline?   1

    The problem of disobedience   2
    A positive approach to discipline   4
    The goal of discipline   7

2 Making a start   10

    Discipline as guidance   11
    Deciding reasonable rules and values   12
    Social training   16
    From egocentricity to altruism   24

3 The problem of authority   28

    Authoritarian and permissive parents   28
    Styles of parenting   29
    Explaining the reasons for discipline   31
    Talking things over and conversation   33
    Losing control   35
    Routines and good habits   36

4 How behaviour is learned   38

    Understanding persistent disobedience   38
    The principle of reinforcement   39
    Strategies for rewarding good behaviour   42
    Strategies for ignoring bad behaviour   46

5	**Making discipline effective**	51
	The importance of timing and consistency	51
	Balancing punishment with positive encouragement	55
	Artificial incentives or reinforcers: tokens and points	57
	Being discriminating with rewards	59
6	**Disobedient children, obedient parents**	61
	The antecedents of tyrannical behaviour	62
	How to regain control	64
7	**Penalties and punishments**	69
	Time-out	70
	Response-cost (fining)	74
	Overcorrection	75
	Reprimands (criticizing/shouting)	75
	Physical punishment	76
	Natural and logical consequences	81
	Combining methods	83
8	**Understanding anger and aggression**	86
	Forms of anger and aggression	86
	The antecedents of aggression	89
	Parental intervention in quarrels	94
9	**Controlling anger and aggression**	97
	Tactics for dealing with aggressive children	97
	Self-help for parents	103
10	**Discipline for teenagers**	112
	Responsibility and freedom	113
	Contracts and negotiations	116
11	**The influence of television**	125
	The influence of television violence	126
	A commonsense approach	128

Contents

Epilogue	131
Appendix: Childcare and discipline questionnaire	132
Bibliography	135

Guidelines

1. The best time to start is at the very beginning. — 10
2. Work out your general strategy on discipline. — 12
3. Have your priorities clear in your own mind. — 13
4. Work out your 'house rules'. — 14
5. Restrict your requests and demands to those that are reasonable and fair; appropriate to your child's age and ability. — 15
6. Happiness and love (alone) are not enough; detailed training is essential. — 18
7. Show your affection and foster your child's love and respect. — 19
8. Set limits for your child. — 22
9. Try to be around enough to encourage your child in his/her efforts to learn about and cope with life. — 25
10. Explain the reasons behind your disciplinary actions. — 30
11. Listen carefully to what your child (or teenager) is saying to you. — 33
12. Prepare your child for life by encouraging personal habits and routines. — 36
13. Ask yourself *what* your child is doing rather than *why* s/he is doing it. — 41
14. Make good behaviour worthwhile. — 42
15. Accentuate the positive. — 45
16. Judge when to ignore your child's misbehaviour. — 46
17. Consequences (positive *or* negative) should follow *promptly* the behaviour they are designed to encourage or discourage. — 52

Guidelines

18	Try to nip misbehaviour in the bud.	53
19	Be consistent.	53
20	Make your requests/demands in a clear, firm and confident manner.	66
21	Tell children what they should do, as well as what they can't do.	69
22	Give your youngster the chance to be responsible by giving him/her responsibility.	113
23	Include your teenager in family discussions.	113
24	Tell your teenager how you feel.	114
25	Refrain from sticking negative 'labels' to your teenager's personality.	115
26	Continue to make firm moral and social demands.	116
27	Teach your teenager the art of compromise.	117
28	Encourage (by example) your teenager to negotiate.	122
29	Keep an eye on things: 'supervision' is not a dirty word.	123
30	Tell yourself you're a good parent.	124

Preface

Discipline without tears

The joys of parents are secret, and so are their griefs.
Francis Bacon, 1597

I have written this book as a guide for all parents and caregivers: those dealing with the day-to-day, 'ordinary' (although trying) transgressions which are an expected part of growing up; and also for those who have to cope with children and/or teenagers who display rebelliousness – remembering that some revolts *are* in a good cause – or other disciplinary difficulties. The points raised should provide a useful spin-off for teachers.

The guidelines discussed here should also be of value to social workers and health visitors who have to help parents experiencing great distress because their child (or teenager) is 'out of control'. They also have to cope with an ever increasing number of child-management cases. There is a fuller understanding today that the majority of worrying incidents are of a relatively minor nature, typically occurring in the context of what parents perceive (rightly or wrongly) as *disciplinary encounters*. Actions that turn out to be inappropriate (sometimes) or abusive are not necessarily malicious in intent, but often impulsive, frustrated, angry and counter-productive attempts to control a child's or teenager's behaviour. Such mismanagement may be due to a lack of 'know how' or a misinterpretation of the events that lead to confrontations.

Unfortunately, in the minds of parents and teachers, discipline is associated mainly with *punishment* and notions of *constraint*. I hope to redress the balance, in this book, by emphasizing the positive aspects of guidance, co-operation and caring which can be the major ingredients in discipline.

Such an approach removes the misery and tension from parent–child relationships and is a recipe for a more mature and healthy outcome to the social training of children and teenagers.

Many of the 'griefs' – the tears referred to in the title of the Preface – come to parents in the course of disciplinary encounters with their children. Their grief often remains secret because of embarrassment. Some parents feel too ashamed to admit to the difficulties they are having with their children or teenagers. There is a common assumption that everyone else finds child management straightforward. Nothing could be further from the truth, as we shall see. The tears also belong to children and teenagers who find themselves at the receiving end of their parents' wrath, indignation or disappointment. They may also be the recipients of painful (sometimes abusive) punishments.

A combination of a *positive* attitude towards children (of whatever age), self-confidence and some know-how, when it comes to disciplinary tactics and strategies, should allow you to pre-empt or ease many of the problems mentioned above. The words 'tactics' and 'strategies' might suggest that I am preparing you for war: a battle of wills between you and your child or teenager. Far from it!

Strategies are about foresight and preparedness. A firm but loving *framework of discipline* helps children to develop their own guidelines and controls so that they can look ahead to the consequences of their actions and 'discipline' themselves. Everyone needs some self-discipline (rules of conduct) in order to adapt his or her needs and desires to those of others, and in order to be a free and happy person. To this end I shall be helping you prepare some broad and positive disciplinary guidelines (thirty in all) for yourself so as to pre-empt or solve the various problems that arise (for all parents) while training their children for life.

Tactics are the special disciplinary – I prefer the word 'teaching' – methods I shall be recommending because of their proven value. Much of the time, of course, parents can, and should, rely on natural, spontaneous reactions to their children's behaviour. But intuition is not enough under certain circumstances, or for children of a particular temperament. Whatever your own situation, it is best to calculate that, unless you have a *choice* of several disciplinary techniques to call on, and have taken time to work out some broad strategy on discipline, you can easily get caught on the hop. It is better to anticipate events than to trail helplessly after them.

If you follow a few tried and tested guidelines, based on extensive research into the rearing and development of children, you will find your job far easier. I often tell my clients to imagine that their child has an L-plate on his or her back to remind them to be patient and tolerant when the child makes a mistake or forgets a lesson. They are, after all, *learners* about life. But it is important to remember that for many young or first-time mothers (and fathers) the same analogy might well apply. The 'L-plate' would refer to their role as *learners* about rearing and disciplining children. They too need help and encouragement. There is evidence that parents are at their best when they do what they have to do with *confidence* and the *support* of their community.

I should like to acknowledge my gratitude to Vivienne Doughty for her skill, and preparedness to risk her eyesight in deciphering my scripts.

Chapter One

Why discipline?

The question of how to discipline children has always been of central importance to the whole enterprise of bringing them up. Given such a responsible, indeed daunting task, it seems paradoxical that parents are not trained to rear their children; and children certainly aren't in a position to bring themselves up properly without help. As parenting involves many quite complex skills, it is not surprising that most mothers and fathers experience occasional difficulties in transforming helpless, unsocialized infants into sensible children and teenagers, and eventually into reasonable adult members of the community.

In order to achieve this goal – referred to by psychologists as *socialization* – they will have to teach their babies and toddlers, and (later) adolescents, many 'lessons'. There will be lessons about the relationships between themselves and others, about social skills and self-restraint; and there will be instructions, requests and demonstrations concerning social requirements and rules. These so-called *norms* reflect society's expectations of what is appropriate, that is to say, *normal* social and moral behaviour. Parents hope that this huge investment of emotion, time and energy in training children – what we call discipline – will have its dividend, eventually, in the emergence of a young adult with good judgement and a mature, responsible outlook. Try comparing your own experiences as a child with your attitudes towards bringing up children as you express them today.

Was bedtime strictly enforced? Were you obliged to attend Sunday school? How often were you expected to brush your teeth? How were lying and stealing dealt with? Was pocket money earned or just given? Were you expected to make your own bed? Were you beaten as a child? If so, by whom and for what offences? Can you recall your thoughts and feelings at the time? How important was school as an influence? Are there any ways in which you would, or do, bring up your own children differently? How have your feelings towards your own parents and teachers changed over the years?

All these questions are concerned with what many people associate with the term discipline – as it affected them. Whatever the disciplinary practices across the generations, it is plain to see that without a reasonable amount of co-operation and compliance from the child, parents wouldn't get far in fulfilling their objectives. Generally speaking, they achieve obedience (albeit sometimes grudgingly) because their children love and respect them, seek their approval, identify with their point of view, and wish to emulate their example.

The problem of disobedience

This is all very well in theory; but disobedience is commonly reported by parents as a problem – in children of all ages. The possibility of disobedience, indeed defiance, arises in three characteristic situations:

- when a young child or teenager is asked to do something, perhaps given an instruction by the parents;
- when he or she is asked to *refrain* from a particular activity;
- when he or she is expected to adhere to general rules of conduct, what might be called the family's 'standing orders'.

There are many circumstances with young children, such as mealtimes, bedtimes or shopping trips, which become fraught with tension and embarrassment, because of the confrontations to which they give rise. Because temper tantrums, aggression and verbal abuse often feature in children's reactions to being thwarted, they will be the subject of my discussions on how to cope more effectively. And, of course, parents themselves are not immune to anger or problems over self-control. I shall recommend ways of keeping cool in the face of severe provocation. The fact is that most parents find discipline one of the most difficult parts of their job; not a few find it an impossible task – especially at particular periods of their children's lives.

Toddlers, for example, can live up to their reputation as members of the species referred to as the 'terrible twos'. They can be exhausting and exasperating, and parents often feel they are not so much raising a lamb as training a tiger. Two- and three-year-olds seem to know just when throwing a tantrum will leave you embarrassed and uncertain and undermine your authority. Say no to sweets in the privacy of your kitchen and they may accept it with scarcely a murmur. Say no at the supermarket checkout and you may have to cope with the whole drama of screams, kicks and sit-ins from your canny three-year-old, while a shopful of people look on, summing up your performance as a parent. It is not easy for parents (and indeed, other caregivers) to know when, how, and how much to discipline. They need to be tough minded as well as lovingly tender and to know when to 'change gear' from one to the other. This is particularly the case in applying discipline to adolescents.

Care and control are the issues where the allegedly 'terrible teens' provide such a daunting challenge. Adolescents are thought of (and often rightly) as disciplinary headaches to their parents. Perhaps *you* are one of those parents who await their child's approaching puberty with apprehension. Do you fear that adolescence is a period when you are likely to lose the closeness, the affection and the degree of parental control that is desirable in your relationship with your son or daughter? If these are your worries you are in good company. Many parents share them; but the defiance and indiscipline (and other disturbing manifestations) associated with adolescence have been much exaggerated.[*] Sadly the many myths about this stage of development could set the stage for the very events you wish to prevent.

*See my *Living with Teenagers*.

If parents expect the worst they are quite likely to get it. Give a dog (so to speak) a bad name, treat him or her accordingly – by having a confrontation or using a suspicious manner – and we are quite likely to trigger a hostile, resentful reaction that confirms our original opinion. We can now self-righteously say, 'I told you so!' And by continuing to treat him or her in a provocative manner we perpetuate a downward spiral of negative actions and reactions: in the case of the teenager, the disciplinary problems we anticipated.

An unpressured, happy early childhood – one that is secured by clear, not oppressive limits – provides the best foundation for *self-discipline* later in life, especially during the testing years of adolescence. Encouraging children to *wish* to be good is more important than *making* them be good. Discipline entirely without tears might be something of a pious hope; but the right approach to discipline *can* minimize the 'griefs' experienced by children (and adults) in the course of developing into mature members of society (or mature and confident parents).

A positive approach to discipline

To do anything really well you have to believe in it. Do you believe in discipline, that children *do* need to be obedient? It all depends on what we mean by the words 'discipline' and 'obedience'. There is a positive *and* negative side to these terms. It could be said to be retrogressive – a return (retreat?) to narrow Victorian child-rearing values - to be writing guidelines on how to encourage obedience and overcome disobedience in the late 1980s. Is it reactionary to be concerned about the issues of parental discipline and authority, and the related aspects of self-discipline and self-control, in these 'enlightened' times of progressive, permissive (some would say *laissez-faire*) child-rearing? The answer to these questions – and I rely on findings from the literature on child development and clinical research – is a resounding 'No'! It is reactionary only when one is concerned about conformity for

A positive approach to discipline

its own sake, obedience as an end in itself, rather than as a *means to an end*.

In the old days, child guidance clinics and, indeed, psychoanalytic couches for adult patients were inundated with problems denoting over-control: neurotic inhibition, anxiety, shyness and many other variations on the themes of repression or suppression. These problems haven't gone away, but they have been dwarfed by difficulties that stem from 'under-control': adolescent and adult excesses due to drug and alcohol abuse; poor self-control of anger; a lack of scruples when it comes to a variety of antisocial actions, ranging from vandalism and violence to child neglect and child abuse. In children too there seems to be an increase in problems relating to antisocial, aggressive conduct and delinquent acts.

Doubtless many social and economic forces have contributed to this trend; but there is good reason to believe that our attitudes to child-rearing play a not insignificant part. Some critics are scathing about the vogue for 'child-centred' schemes that fail (allegedly) to provide young people with even the rudiments of human culture; they believe that contemporary views of childhood and childcare are unequal to the task of producing in children such socially desirable qualities as competence, co-operation, responsiblity, social sensitivity and moral awareness. If such criticisms are valid, is a sterner, more restrictive approach either desirable or likely to be effective?

If you read old childcare manuals you soon become aware of a 'pendulum' of fashion swinging one way, then another. Confusingly, parents were advised to do X; then, after perhaps a generation X was out, it was best to do Y. Nowadays we can rely on research studies for at least some evidence about the desirability and effectiveness of this or that approach, and about the influence of certain styles of parenting on the child's development and wellbeing. In the end, however, child-rearing is very much about values – and these are very individual matters, relating to one's attitudes, beliefs and style of living.

Why discipline?

What is interesting is that the most effective child rearing practices (as far as these things are measurable) appear to represent a 'golden mean' between the *extremes* suggested by successive fashions. For example, until a few generations ago, children were not given the freedom to express themselves and their individuality. Their conformity to convention was developed largely through fear of punishment (which often meant physical punishment). Sadly, it was not only their wilder impulses that were sternly checked but, all too often, (as clinical psychologist Allan Fromme puts it), their 'creative imagination, curiosity, intellectual expressiveness, and capacity for enjoyment'. Children weren't allowed to share the adult world to the same degree as they do now. In many ways (and in most homes and schoolrooms) it was a case of children being seen but not heard.

When a reaction set in, the experts (as so often tends to be the case with childcare issues) went over the top. The 'permissive era' had begun for many parents and children. There were many exceptions, of course; but there was a pervasive attitude – largely based on a misinterpretation of Sigmund Freud's psychoanalytic theorizing – that children should be inhibited as little as possible. 'Interfere as little as possible with nature' was the watchword. Resonances of some of the ideas of Jean Jacques Rousseau had reached our century and bedded down well with 'new' ideologies about childcare. Children were accorded the intensive, individual right of self-expression.

With the coming of a child-centred approach to discipline, the old obsessive concern with orderly habits and unfailing obedience was discarded. Unfortunately, for many parents the alternative to heavy-handed, autocratic childcare practices meant an excessively idealistic (or self-indulgent) *laissez-faire* attitude to a very serious business, and there are critics who believe we are now reaping the harvest of our 'permissive' ways (see page 16). Certainly for many mothers the price of freeing their children from the oppressive atmosphere of yesteryear was yet a further form of oppression for themselves when freedom was overdone. I shall return to this matter in chapter 6.

Allan Fromme makes the point that good discipline takes account of the child's *emotional life*, which we know much more about today. We have come to appreciate that we cannot expect children to live by our adult standards too early, or too quickly, without doing them harm; but nor should we expect them to socialize themselves. We are, or should be, much more willing to allow children to enjoy the special world of childhood without forcing them into premature adulthood. This does not mean opting out of positive training or the setting of limits. It does mean foregoing regimentation.

This approach places a great burden on parents, since it requires tolerance and endless patience; but it can bring out the best in the child. As I hope to demonstrate later, by far the largest majority of infants are biased towards being social rather than antisocial. The skill is to encourage that tendency and have them well and truly on your side.

The goal of discipline

So what does one do? The starting point is a redefinition of the goal of discipline, and here we might heed the words of Allan Fromme:

Ideally, we should help the child develop the ability eventually to discipline himself. By self-discipline we mean the judicious guidance of our desires and impulses through the elaborate filter of convention so as to obtain the maximum amount of self-satisfaction and social approval. In other words, we learn to fulfill the demands of social living without personal resentment. This is a big order – so big that it's safe to say we only partially achieve this in ourselves, to say nothing of our children. However, we try to give this to our children nonetheless.

I hope to have established the point that it is not necessary to adopt the apocalyptic views of events put forward by the more sombre critics, nor to deserve the dismissive label 'puritanical' in order to believe that there are very good reasons why parents *have to enforce rules*. The point is that they should be *reasonable* rules. They should also be essential:

- for the child's (and later the teenager's) safety – the youngster has to learn to avoid dangers;
- for harmony within the family – a disobedient child or revolting adolescent sets the scene for an unhappy home and disharmony between the parents;
- for the social life of the family – spoiled, noisy, aggressive, destructive 'brats' are not welcome in other people's homes and contribute to the social isolation of their parents;
- for children's ability to concentrate and thus benefit from school, as well as for the self-discipline required to achieve success in a chosen field of endeavour;
- for children's and teenagers' wellbeing – they have to learn rules, roles and skills in order to develop self-esteem and self-control, and these attributes are, in the end, liberating and also signs of growing maturity;
- for the wellbeing of the community in which we reside – a society without rules or norms about courteous behaviour, mutual obligations and co-operation would be brutish and possibly short-lived.

Many of the more worrying disciplinary problems of childhood and adolescence involve *moral* rules, and it is when children break these rules that parents become most perturbed. Youngsters are forbidden to lie, steal, cheat and hurt others. You cannot always be on hand (and nor would you wish to be) to monitor your child. Eventually your voice, and other voices which speak for society, must be taken inside the psyche of the child so that what he or she obeys is their own voice of conscience.

Through learning, children acquire not only their parents' moral code but also a willingness to act in accordance with the rules. Going back to those first commands and prohibitions on which (among other things) conscience is founded, it is apparent that some babies heed them more readily and consistently than others, and that some parents convey them more effectively than others.

You may be surprised to know that there are as many as four different components to moral behaviour:

- *resistance to temptation*, which is the braking mechanism against misbehaviour, even when unobserved;
- *guilt*, the acute emotional discomfort that follows transgression of the rules and leads to confession, reparation or blaming oneself;
- *altruism*, which represents acts of kindness, generosity, sympathy and service to others;
- *moral insight* and *belief*, terms which cover all the things people think and say about morality, including their willingness to blame others who do wrong.

Some older children and adults are highly moral in all these respects, and others are scarcely, if at all, moral in any of them. Many people seem to concentrate on particular components of moral behaviour. Certain children find it easier to resist temptation than others; certain parents more effectively foster strong consciences in their offspring than others (see page 51). When it is a matter of discipline, it is important to begin as you intend to continue.

Chapter Two

Making a start

You need to begin to develop your 'philosophy' of discipline from the child's birth. If you delay it until he/she is two or three years old, it is probably because you are subconsciously thinking of discipline as something unpleasant rather than a *positive* way of giving direction and equipping the child for life.

Guideline 1: The best time to start is at the very beginning

If you have your doubts and are uncertain about what line to take, or when to start, you are one of a multitude of parents. Discipline must be one of the more emotive words in the language, guaranteed to raise hackles wherever or whenever the subject is broached. It is certainly one of the most misunderstood terms, and therefore also guaranteed to lead to disagreement, even (or perhaps especially) among the so-called experts.

Because for many parents the word discipline has the unhappy connotation of punishment and repression, they have been half afraid to begin to discipline their young children. They have been concerned about damaging them or losing their affection. This is regrettable, since discipline is, or should be, a positive process of training and parental leadership which helps children and teenagers come to terms with the world outside the family.

Discipline as guidance

It should help you if you think of discipline as a means to an end, *not* an end in itself. Essentially, discipline is about 'steering' the child through the shallows and rapids of life, by example and guidance, and with the encouragement that fosters growth and development. A disciple is one who learns from or voluntarily follows a leader. But a child is not a voluntary recruit to the processes of discipline, but a sometimes reluctant participant in them. Parents and teachers are the leaders, and the child is expected to obey them because they 'know best' what is right for the individual and the society he/she is being prepared or (as some would have it) fitted for.

The words 'fitted for' hint at the reasons for disobedience. Children, in growing up and being socialized, are made to give up much that is pleasurable – not least, some of their individuality – for the sake of principles which are not always made clear to them, or may be obscure even to the person demanding obedience. If anything has changed in the attitude of modern theorists towards discipline and obedience, it is *not* the fundamental issue of whether discipline is necessary, since almost everyone would agree that some discipline is indispensible. The changes are about *how* to discipline and the reasons for requiring obedience to certain rules. The change in the ways of disciplining has been most evident in the gradual erosion of absolutist, authoritarian and punitive methods of discipline. Many parents have become more democratic in their treatment of children. They have slightly relaxed their demands for absolute obedience to the rules and do not think they are demeaning themselves by giving reasons for their 'do's' and 'don'ts'.

Unfortunately a child's behaviour may be misunderstood or misinterpreted through what is called faulty 'attribution'. Some parents attribute incorrect or erroneous motives, desires or ideas to their children. For example, although babies cry for all sorts of reasons – hunger, pain, discomfort and loneliness – they *do not* cry to 'get at' their parents. Yet this is how crying in infants is sometimes interpreted: the child is being naughty; naughtiness is punished; smacking is how I was punished as a child; so I smack my baby. This is wholly wrong and dangerous, because a faulty attribution leads to an unjust retribution! Discipline during infancy is *positive* guidance, the establishment of routines and rules. Penalties (sadly) come later.

Guideline 2: Work out your general strategy on discipline.

Deciding reasonable rules and values

Both parents need to think out their attitudes to discipline and discuss them fully. It is important to present a *united front*; only you can decide on the values (and the rules, routines and standards that underlie them) which are important in your family, and therefore worth insisting on. Don't get into the situation where one of you has to act the 'bad guy' while the other is always the 'good guy'.

If you cannot agree on matters of discipline, your child will soon spot the differences in outlook and drive a coach and horses through your serenity. If the father is trying to instil good table manners while the mother is arguing, 'What does it matter, so long as she eats?', or the mother is trying to set up a sensible bedtime routine while father says 'Another half-hour won't hurt', mealtimes and bedtimes will soon turn into problem areas. Children soon learn the motto 'Divide and rule'.

The same applies to the single parent if he or she is inconsistent. As I will show later, the child may play off that side of you that is exhausted and wishes to take the 'line of least resistance', against that part of you that wishes to make a stand on an important matter of principle.

There are three issues you have to sort out at different ages and phases of your child's development, and they involve the following questions:

- *What* expectations should I have; what rules are important

Deciding reasonable rules and values

for my son or daughter at this stage of his or her development? What requests based on these rules and expectations can I reasonably make?
- *Why* am I choosing these particular requirements: do they make sense? I must remember to include positive encouragements and requirements, *not* only a series of 'don'ts' and 'mustn'ts'. Are they designed for my child's *safety*, *security of mind* and *social training*, rather than just for *my* convenience?
- *How* am I going to encourage and, if it becomes necessary, enforce these requirements and rules?

The *what* question provides us with the next guideline:

Guideline 3: Have your priorities clear in your own mind.

You could think of your child's behaviour as falling into three colour codes: green, amber and red.

- *Green* is the 'go-ahead' code for the type of behaviour you want from your children, the actions you always remember to praise and encourage: sharing toys with another child, perhaps, or going to bed without a prolonged fuss. As your children get older you will probably want to encourage them towards a more unselfish view of the world by pointing out that their rights have to be balanced against the rights of others - and that includes their parents. If you use the green code consistently the idea should be well rooted by the time they go to school.
- *Amber* is for 'caution' behaviour, which you don't encourage but tolerate because your child is still learning and making mistakes: something like digging holes in the lawn with his spade or hurling her toys across the room in a moment of fury. Any sort of stress such as moving house, illness or upset in the family may cause the child to take a temporary step backwards in behaviour. Be understanding if he or she suddenly starts wetting the bed or crying for attention following a bad dream in the night.

- *Red* is definite 'stop' (No! No!) behaviour which needs to be curbed as soon as possible. Obviously anything which could be dangerous for him or her, or others, has a red code: running into the road, climbing the railway fence, attacking the toddler next door with his teeth.

I will discuss the priorities for older children and teenagers in chapter 10.

With young children, teaching obedience to rules requires knowledge of three matters:

- Does he or she know *what* to do?
- Does he or she know *how* to do it?
- Does he or she know *when* to do it?

Guideline 4: Work out your 'house rules'.

Don't devise a long list of rules for the sake of having rules: make sure they serve a purpose – to enhance your child's safety, wellbeing and steady (not hurried) progress towards maturity. Ask yourself:

- Are the rules necessary?
- Are they simple?
- Are they fair?
- Does my child understand them?
- Does he or she know what will happen if the rules are broken?
- Do I (and my partner) apply the rules fairly?

It may help, with the older child, to write or type out the *house rules* (the 'standing orders') and post them up in the kitchen or elsewhere. Parents usually have a *general rule* for day-to-day convenience and safety: this requires a reasonable ratio of obedient to disobedient responses to parental requests, instructions and commands. You are probably doing well with toddlers if you achieve a success rate of between 50 and 70 per cent.

If we accept that there are excellent reasons for requiring young children to show obedience to their parents, this does

Deciding reasonable rules and values

not mean that parents should ask anything, or too much, of their children. Some requests or demands are reasonable and fair, but others certainly might not be so because they fail to take into account the child's right to his/her needs and point of view, or because they are inappropriate to his/her level of development. To ask a child to get dressed is a reasonable requirement of a seven-year-old but not of a two-year-old. In making demands of a child you need to ensure that the request is appropriate to his or her age and ability, and that you are not expecting too much.

Guideline 5: Restrict your requests and demands to those that are:

- reasonable and fair;
- appropriate to your child's age and ability.

If you have any doubts about what is or is not appropriate for a child of a given age, then seek advice from your doctor, a child psychologist or health visitor, or from other parents, particularly those whose children are older than yours. Don't forget that there are many good books on child development (see Bibliography).

Many parents – as part of their 'standing orders' – insist on good manners. This is not a trivial or old-fashioned goal in child-rearing. After all, saying 'please' and 'thank you', offering a helping hand, giving a seat to an elderly or disabled person, are the outward and visible signs that we feel that other people and their rights matter. The actions themselves may be insignificant in themselves, but what they show about our *concern for others*, whether they are friends or strangers, is very important. Without a generally accepted code of manners life would become thoroughly uncouth and unpleasant, so parents need to pass this on to their children.

The best way of teaching your child good manners is by consistent example. If you see a mother yelling at her child, 'Hey you – get in here!', you won't be surprised to find the child has awful manners. A father who elbows his way to the front of a queue, dragging his toddler behind him, is likely to produce the sort of child who pushes others out of the way to grab the best cakes.

If you treat other people, including your child, with consideration, you will need very little in the way of formal manners teaching. Of course, you will have to prompt, remind and explain occasionally. Children start off as self-centred little beings and they do not naturally think of the other person. As they get older and identify with you, they will want to copy your style of behaviour. Of course, you will not be waiting for your child's fifth or sixth birthday before you begin putting across the idea of good manners. This goes hand in hand with teaching them speech ('Don't forget to say "thank you" '), teaching him self-restraint ('Ask nicely. Don't grab'), teaching social skills ('Say "hello" to aunty. She said "hello" to you'), teaching her to eat in the proper way ('Close your mouth when you are eating and don't gulp your food'), and so on.

Social training

Parents and teachers usually judge children's behaviour by whether it fits in with the usual standards – moral, emotional, social and intellectual – set by the society in which they live. They have a picture of the sort of person the child should be and of the society he is being fitted for, and they aim to civilize an infant 'barbarian', ruled by his wants and emotions, into that person. If he fails dismally to adjust to the norm, or fights hard against it, we tend to think that he is maladjusted. There is a problem here for liberal parents. The last thing they wish to do is to squash and destroy a child's individuality. Fortunately, there is little chance of that except in extreme cases. Slavish conformity is not what we want of a child. But growing up and learning how she ought to feel and behave, what she ought to value, means that she has to give up doing just as she pleases. Obviously she will often clash with the adults who are grooming her for life.

However, though children often act in ways which seem unreasonable and troublesome to their elders, from their point of view, adult behaviour is often just as unreasonable and incomprehensible. A mother insists on her small son's going to bed at a certain time, in spite of all his protests, because she knows he needs enough sleep to keep healthy and alert; but in his view, she is insisting that he gives up his happy play, cutting him off from the rest of the family, for no good reason. A girl who pummels a destructive little brother who ruins her toys and finds she is the one who gets into trouble feels hurt and angry. 'Bad' behaviour can be a furious reaction to adult behaviour, which is beyond the child's understanding.

A survey of some 2000 British families by the psychiatrist Michael Rutter showed that nearly all reported a number of undesirable forms of behaviour in their children, but parents varied in the amount of 'bad' behaviour they could tolerate. Some parents are better at turning a blind eye than others. Teachers, who have to cope with a large group of children, are likely to regard aggressive or disruptive youngsters as problems and overlook those who are quiet and withdrawn because, in their terms, they are 'well behaved'. However, a psychologist might be worried about an unusually subdued or docile child. Whatever direction these problems (often the consequence of faulty discipline) take, the children – be they overly assertive or submissive – are seldom happy.

Actually, happiness is something of a treacherous word in child-rearing. Some parents, in their understandable desire to make their children happy, give in to them and let them have everything they ask for. Others do this misguidedly because they want to 'make up' (i.e. compensate) for the child's handicap. Such a policy usually leads to the opposite of happiness. Haim Ginott observes:

> Happiness ... is not a destination; it is a manner of travelling. Happiness is not an end in itself. It is a

by-product of working, playing, loving and living. Living, by necessity, involves delay between desire and fulfilment, between plan and realization. In other words, it involves frustration and the endurance of frustration.

There is another popular myth: as long as you love your child all will be well; nature will take its course, the bud will flower, the flower will bloom. If the notion of the sufficiency of love leads to the neglect of social training, it is likely that the young plant (to continue the metaphor) will be blighted.

Guideline 6: Happiness and love (alone) are not enough; detailed training is essential.

It is important to take time for training and teaching children essential skills and habits. If parents do not find time for such training they will spend more time scolding and correcting at a later stage.

A respect for rules and a reasonable degree of conformity to norms do not just 'happen' because there is a pleasant home atmosphere. Conformity of behaviour to specific or particular situations is more likely to depend on the *sanctions attached by parents to those particular situations* than on the general parent–child relationship. The minutiae of discipline merit serious attention.

Nevertheless, the general principles concerning relationships still apply. A loving bond fuels the child's efforts to learn. It can almost be considered a law of human nature that punishment leads to self-control only when the child is on the side of the person punishing.

Mutual respect and affection

The first and most crucial step in training children to be social beings takes place when they develop a *willingness* to do as they are told. What they learn will depend upon the content of their parents' demands, but the initial *disposition* towards compliance may be critical for the effectiveness of all further attempts at discipline and social training.

Far from being antagonistic to the requirements of society – as was assumed by many theorists – infants are genetically biased towards the *social* and towards displaying social behaviours. This is scarcely surprising; human beings have evolved as a social species. The family is a microcosm of social existence for which our young are pre-adapted. Thus a disposition towards obedience, in fact towards socialization in general, is the product of proper social development rather than the result of a rigorous and heavy-handed training regime.

Many a parent struggling with an unruly child may be surprised to hear this, but as the developmental psychologist Mary Ainsworth observes:

> Clearly, as a child matures increasing parental intervention will be necessary. A child will not conform 'naturally' to all the rules of his or her parents or society, no matter how benevolent the home environment may be. It is the initial disposition to comply with which we are concerned, and this seems to be a 'natural emergent'.

What, then, does all this mean? We know that most children *are* disposed to comply. But you can help the process if you show love and appreciation; this will assist them to internalize your guidelines.

Guideline 7: Show your affection and foster your child's love and respect.

Of course it will be difficult for the child – the recipient of parental love – to appreciate affection and respond to it unless it is *outwardly* demonstrated. Discipline will be effective only if there is a two-way bond of affection and respect between parent(s) and child.

If children fear that their parents will stop loving them when they are naughty, they soon absorb the idea of what they *must* do. The idea of what they *ought* to do is more subtle and will come to them only if they love and trust their parents enough to want to be like them. The more affection there is between you, the more notice your children will take of everything you tell them. Remember to make it clear that, however cross or disappointed you are over something he/she has done, it is only that particular piece of behaviour you dislike. It may seem obvious to you that you don't love them any less, but it isn't obvious to them – especially if you are in the habit of saying, 'You've been naughty. I don't love you anymore.'

Internalization and self-restraint

Parents cannot always be on the spot to point out the sensible course of action, to remind children about the rules or to enforce them. So the 'markers' of good judgement and the rules that are really important must become so ingrained that children have their own discretion and a conscience to 'remind' them of right and wrong. Self-discipline begins to take over so that children come more and more to behave reasonably, even when there is no one present to tell them what to do.

Of course this will not happen overnight. First comes the young child's attachment to parents – a growing bond of affection, respect and loyalty. Parents who nurture this bond are the most important people in the child's world, and they are taken as *models* to identify with and imitate.

When parents criticize or disapprove of what their children do (when unacceptable), the fact that their offspring love and respect them puts them on the *same side* as their parents; it means that they will take what is being said seriously, and will emulate them by beginning to criticize their bad behaviour *themselves*! They take into themselves that judgement of what is unacceptable behaviour ('internalization'), a step on the road to forming a conscience.

Social training

And what an important step it is! Social adjustment (adaptation) begins to take hold when children try to restrain their impulses because they know others will disapprove. She wants to take biscuits from the kitchen but she doesn't because she knows she will get into trouble. He may long to skip an afternoon's school and play on the swings instead, but the thought of disapproving parents weighs more heavily than the thought of a couple of hours' fun.

Children who are alienated by parental rejection, disaffected by continuous and severe punishment, do not identify with their parents' point of view when they are being disciplined, and are therefore less likely to agree with the criticism being made and less liable to 'internalize' the judgement.

The internalization of rules, values and judgements is an important part of social and moral development. On the one hand there are the conventional rules of good manners and of correct behaviour; on the other, the rules concerning sympathy and respect for others, keeping faith, honesty, and so on. The latter are moral issues. As the psychologist Derek Wright puts it:

> If we find the rules of a particular activity uncongenial or impossible to keep, we can, at least in principle, contract out and play a different game. However uncongenial and difficult moral rules may be to keep, we cannot contract out.... Moral rules are foundational in the sense that they are concerned with the maintenance of, for instance, trust, mutual help and justice in human relationships. Unless these exist in some measure it becomes virtually impossible to continue any social activity. Moral rules form the yardstick against which we evaluate the rules of any particular activity. It is therefore not surprising that, though conventions and customs vary widely from one society to another, basic moral principles apparently do not.

In the process whereby a child comes to act in accordance with the rules and values of society, becoming eventually a reasonably self-controlled, inner-directed member of the community, one of the first steps is the development of *self-restraint*. Children learn self-restraint as part of the process by which they learn the values and attitudes of the society in which they will move. They begin to associate certain forbidden actions and dangerous situations – running impulsively into the road or snatching another child's toy – with disapproval or punishment, so they avoid them; they are afraid of angering their parents or getting hurt. Children and, later, teenagers have to learn to put a brake on their impulses, to tame their desires. You can help them.

Guideline 8: Set limits for your child.

Setting limits

Children whose parents set firm limits for them grow up better adjusted, with greater self-esteem, than those who are allowed to get away with behaving any way they like. What do I mean by limits? I have in mind *that point* beyond which parents are no longer flexible, don't allow their children a certain amount of leeway, are not prepared to overlook or make light of mistakes or misdemeanours. In essence they are saying: 'Beyond this point you *cannot* go!' It may be a boundary drawn for the toddler's safety ('You are *not* to go out of the front gate'); it may be to do with the teenager's wellbeing ('You do an hour's homework' or 'You have to tell me who you're out with and where you'll be').

Children may make a fuss when the limits are set down and insisted on, but there is a great deal of evidence to show that children and teenagers realize their parents are firm because they care (see page 116). They know, deep down, that they cannot cope alone. They need to know someone has charge of their lives, then they can build from a base of safety and security. Children who get their own way all the time interpret *laissez-faire* permissiveness as indifference. They

Social training

feel nothing they do is important enough for their parents to bother about. So, even if you have to cope with a few tears and sulks, don't let them get you down.

There is, as always, a balance. Parents can overdo the restraints, setting narrow 'Victorian' limits rather than sensibly broad ones. It is here that your values and ideas about preparing children (i.e. guiding and training them) for life need to be worked out clearly and communicated to your youngster in the form of reasons. When children *overdo* self-restraint, problems arise which can sometimes affect their future happiness. If they are strongly and exclusively attached to domineering parents who set impossibly high standards and are deeply 'hurt' when their offspring fail to live up to them, it is probable that they will acquire a sense of conscience so severe and restrictive that their spontaneity and emotional life will be crippled and much of their creative energy will remain unused. They may find it hard to adapt or compromise, so that others find them too rigid. If they have overprotective parents, always worried and fearful, they may not develop the confidence they need, and become shy and timid, unable to take responsibility and always looking to others to take the lead.

A supplementary guideline to setting limits for children might be: 'Set limits or boundaries for yourself'. Your child's best interests and your own should converge if you do. Mary Georgina Boulton observes that women with pre-school children, in order to restore a sense of control in their lives and cope with their workload, need to create a structure to their work. One way of doing this is by imposing boundaries, with regard to both *time and space*, which children and childcare are not allowed to cross. Boulton quotes R.V., a mother of three small children who created a time boundary:

> I would like to give them more of my time. Instead of putting them down for the afternoon, I'd like to be able to do something with them. But I do think if I don't have a break, then before long I shall blow my temper. Their afternoon sleep is very important to *me*. Once I get them up from their rest, we go off to the lake and

feed the ducks or we go to friends. But that break is important to *me*.

N.L., a mother of two, created territorial limits:

The living room is the room where they mustn't take their toys. Normally during the day I keep it shut because that's the place we like to keep clean, in case someone happens to come over and doesn't want to be knee-deep in children.

Women also created important opportunities for the many tasks of childcare to be handled through *routines* (see page 36), another example where what is good for the child can be good for the parent.

From egocentricity to altruism

Infants go through a period of being completely self-centred. For a while they are 'egocentric' – so self-centred that they seem to be interested only in themselves and their own point of view. When the toddler makes endless demands on his mother, he is oblivious to her exhaustion. When he pinches his baby brother he seems indifferent to the infant's distress. Don't worry: this type of behaviour is a normal part of children's development, but they usually leave it behind as they grow up.

When your small child behaves selfishly she is not deliberately disregarding the other person's feelings, she is simply unaware of them. So far she is only able to see things from her own point of view. A baby's world is centred on herself. There is no distinction between 'me' and 'other people' so she does not realize that the world outside is separate from her.

When she first begins to talk, she uses two different types of speech: *egocentric speech*, a kind of monologue, when she chatters on without bothering to know whom she is speaking to or even whether they are listening; and *socialized speech*, a sign of growing maturity and decentring, when she tries to carry on a conversation, reacting to what the other person says. Many of the difficulties children get into as they begin to explore the immediate environment of their home happen because they do not know enough to realize what will occur if they, for example, put their hands in a rose bush or pick up a shining splinter of glass. But some accidents happen because of their egocentric tendency to think of themselves as invulnerable. For instance, a child may become so fascinated by watching a car backing up the drive that she fails to realize the danger of being in its way.

You will see the gradual development of a less self-centred view in your child's play. If he is to play successfully with others he must be aware of them as persons like himself, with feelings and rights which must be recognized and adjusted to. He has to give up his egocentricity and develop the beginnings of a more altruistic point of view. You may hear the stirrings of the inner voice of altruism as your three-year-old says things like: 'Oh, all right, you haven't had a turn; you have a go on the swing' or 'I'll lead the dog next time; you have a go now'. You can facilitate (and 'facilitating' is a disciplinary 'technique') this pro-social tendency by remembering our next guideline:

Guideline 9: Try to be around enough to encourage your child in his/her efforts to learn about and cope with life.

Rudolf Dreikurs has observed that encouragement implies faith in the child *as she is*, not in her potentiality. Children misbehave when they are discouraged and believe they cannot succeed by useful means. They need encouragement as a plant needs water, especially in being guided towards *pro-social* actions.

Let us be clear about what we mean by pro-social (altruistic) behaviour? Generally speaking the term covers actions such as comforting, helping, sharing, reassuring and defending. Children below three years of age can show some forms of pro-social behaviour, especially after (approximately) twenty months. At an older phase – for example, children aged four and five years in pre-school classes – they have been observed sharing, helping or comforting about once every 10–12 minutes on average. Boys and girls show about the same amount of pro-social behaviour. Although young children (say, from eighteen months to six years) can be quarrelsome (as we shall see in chapter 8), pro-social actions may be seen in some 10–20 per cent of all social contacts.

A study of mothers' reports of their four- and seven-year-olds over a four-week period indicated an act of helping (excluding regular duties) every day or so. Boys and girls did not differ. It was rare for mothers not to respond when they observed an act of helpfulness by their child. The vast majority of such actions were 'rewarded' verbally, by thanking or praising, or physically, by smiling or hugging. If children were not helpful (when their mothers thought helpfulness was appropriate) it was rare for the mothers to overlook their negligence.

The research of Jerome Bruner, an eminent child-developmental psychologist, demonstrates how important *play* is as a vehicle for teaching children the conventions of their community. So do find opportunities to play with your child, and also the time, occasionally, to observe him/her at play with other children. Children of three (for example) can be highly aware of, and sensitive to, the fairness of co-operating and sharing, but they may not be so good at returning to these conditions after, say, a quarrel. You can often get them back on track by suggesting that they take turns at riding the tricycle or that they make the Lego building a joint effort.

In doing this try not to become too intrusive. Whenever your child is unselfish, helpful or sensitive to how others feel, reward her with words of praise and encouragement. When she is egocentric, you can point out the injustices, cruelties and thoughtlessness which arise from her limited capacity to feel for others. Encourage her to put herself in the other person's shoes with explanations and reasons along the lines of: 'How would you feel if . . .?'

This suggestion leads us on to the subject of the next chapter: the issue of how one uses authority. Are you secure enough as a parent, comfortable enough with your authority to use it empathetically – firmly when the occasion calls for it, lightly when it is appropriate to be tolerant?

Chapter Three

The problem of authority

A common problem for adults both at home and at work is how to wield authority and/or respond to it. Parents have (or should have) authority over their children and this constitutes both a responsibility *and* a burden. Sadly, some parents duck out of both of these.

I have seen many toddlers comprehensively 'running' their own and seemingly their parents' lives, but they didn't look very happy getting their own way. Children (and teenagers) are, by definition, immature; they need and welcome the security of a 'sure touch' on the part of their mothers and fathers – a sense of authority fairly and kindly expressed. There is evidence that as pupils they also want this from their teachers.

Authoritarian and permissive parents

There are different styles of parenting. Not all of them provide that 'sure touch' – that firm but gentle control of the rudder which is what gives the child his or her sense of direction. As always, there are extremes. At one extreme, according to the psychologist Diana Baumrind, are restrictive or 'authoritarian' parents. Detailed investigations reveal these to be adults who attempt to shape, control and judge the behaviour and attitudes of their children according to unbending standards of conduct, usually absolute standards, often determined by theological considerations. Such parents value obedience as a virtue and favour punitive, forceful measures to curb self-will at those points where the child's actions or beliefs conflict with what they think is proper conduct. They believe in indoctrinating the child with such values as respect for authority, respect for work, and respect for the preservation of traditional order. They do not encourage verbal give and take, believing that the child should accept unquestioningly that *they* know best.

What, in general, is the effect of such rigid parenting? Studies suggest that autocratic, strict (i.e. undemocratic) parental domination tends to produce conforming children while (in the process) undermining their initiative. Such children turn out to be rather passive, colourless, unimaginative and incurious – burdened, in addition, with shyness and a sense of inadequacy. They usually lack self-reliance and the ability to cope realistically with their problems, and later on fail (or are slow) to accept adult responsibilities. In addition they are apt to be submissive and extremely biddable; far too willing, also, to withdraw from situations they find difficult.

An extremely 'permissive' parent, on the other hand, attempts to behave in a non-punitive, accepting and affirmative manner towards children's impulses, desires and actions; always to consult with them about policy decisions and give explanations for family rules; to make few demands for household responsibility and orderly behaviour; to present himself/herself to them as someone to call upon for help and company as they wish, rather than as an active 'disciplinary agent' responsible for shaping or altering behaviour. Such parents allow children to regulate their own activities as much as possible; avoid the exercise of control and do not encourage their children to obey externally defined standards. Over-permissive parents attempt always to use reason instead of overt authority to accomplish their goals.

Styles of parenting

Research into disciplinary techniques suggests that the extremes of permissiveness and restrictiveness entail risks. A blend of permissiveness and forcefulness, combined with warmth and encouragement, fits the recommendations of child-rearing specialists who are concerned with fostering the sort of children who are socially outgoing, friendly, creative and reasonably independent and self-assertive. Warm, loving and consistent discipline, in which reasons are given (when the child can understand them), is thought to produce the rational sort of 'obedience' rather than the mindless and emotionally dependent following of orders.

The balance is perhaps best illustrated in the philosophy of what Diana Baumrind calls the 'authoritative parent'. This kind of parent (let us take the mother as our example) attempts to direct her child's activities in a rational manner determined by the issues involved in particular disciplinary situations. She values both the child's self-expression and his respect for authority, work and the like; she appreciates both independent self-will and disciplined conformity. Therefore, she exerts firm control at points where she and the child diverge in viewpoint, but does not hem in the child with endless restrictions. She recognizes her own special rights as an adult, but also the child's individual interests and special characteristics. The authoritative parent affirms the child's present qualities, but also sets standards for future conduct. She uses reason as well as power to achieve her objectives. She does not base her decisions solely on the consensus of the group or the individual child's desires, but also does not regard herself as infallible or divinely inspired.

Diana Baumrind found that authoritative parents are most likely to facilitate the development of competence and self-reliance in young children by enhancing responsible, purposive and independent behaviour. These parents are notable for encouraging verbal give-and-take, and share with the child the reasoning behind their policy. This provides us with our next guideline.

Guideline 10: Explain the reasons behind your disciplinary actions.

Giving explanations is vital for children's training because discipline is not merely the administration of a ragbag of cuddles, cuffs, sermons and lectures. It is about something infinitely subtle: moral and social development. In the old days people spoke of the development of character. With this in mind you might try to point out the consequences (effects) of your children's behaviour for themselves and for others. This helps to develop *empathy* – the ability to see things from the other's point of view in addition to one's own.

Explaining the reasons for discipline

When children were expected to be unquestioningly compliant, parents would suppress undesirable behaviour without discussing the whys and wherefores of their prohibitions. It would have been thought of as demeaning their authority to have to explain their actions. Such a policy had (and has) its risks; the forbidden becomes tempting – especially if there seems no good reason for a restriction. Indeed, in many cases *there may be no meaning* in the demands being made of children. A rule is a rule is a rule ... If standards are set in concrete, there is no way of teaching children that there *are* times to be flexible, when special circumstances demand it. Also, rules are meaningless to a child if they do not have a rationale.

Scolding a child for being 'a bad boy' or 'a dirty girl' is not educative; telling a child to do something 'because I say so' teaches her nothing useful. Nowadays a thoughtful parent will say, 'Don't pick up things from the floor and put them in your mouth; they are dirty and might make you ill. Remember how nasty it was the last time you were sick?' or 'Don't leave your doll at the top of the stairs, because someone might trip over it and fall to the bottom. They would hurt themselves.'

In practice, however, there are drawbacks, no matter how sound the advice seems in theory. Timing is one consideration. Providing explanations for discipline will *not* necessarily have an immediate effect on children's obedience. But rest assured: in the longer term, giving reasons will certainly foster their compliance and, most important, the sort of reliability you can depend upon even when you are not there to keep an eye on things.

There is another potential drawback; it has to do with the fluent child's love of (or abuse of) debate. Timing is of the essence in obedience training, and children (at home and in the classroom) are adept at delaying and diversionary tactics. You may find yourself in the midst of a lengthy disputation about the rights and wrongs of a particular request you made ('But *you* said another five minutes, mum!'). Such discussions not only take an inordinate amount of time (a subtle form of disobedience), but they are subversive because they are so rewarding to the child. Explain what is wanted. If you are sure he/she understands what is required, don't argue, don't keep repeating yourself. Take action! *Later* you could explain again the reasons for your action.

Not all disciplinary abuses in the home are the severe deprivations or punishments that deform the lives of some children. Some arise from an insensitivity to the child's curiosity, his/her intelligence and feelings. Often there is no intention to frustrate the child; the rejections – such as not listening to or fobbing off the child – may be the consequences of the parent's being too busy with chores or being tired and irritable after a day's work, and so forth. After all, parents have rights too!

Children have a knack of choosing the most inconvenient or embarrassing times for their Socratic dialogues. However, questioning is a legitimate and necessary part of their adaptation to life. Questioning is by way of being a bargain: 'You are asking me to give something up; well then, give me a good reason for doing so.' It is part of the vital learning process, especially for the development of a value system and conscience. It is not that parents occasionally, and doubtless understandably, have to switch off the seemingly inexhaustible stream of 'whys'. The point is that some parents do it habitually.

Talking things over and conversation

As children grow older and more articulate, it becomes easier to reason with them and they are better able (if you find the time) to explain their needs to you. However, from the moment they can talk, they should be encouraged to explain why they have done something you told them not to do and given time to do so, especially when they are still clumsy or slow with words. Talking things over with them, however simply, will help them to think for themselves and learn to look ahead to the possible consequences of their actions.

Guideline 11: Listen carefully to what your child (or teenager) is saying to you.

Many parents do just this; they appreciate that communication is a vital two-way process. But far too many listen only rarely to their children and have little to say to them that is not punitive.

A study carried out at Aberdeen University discovered rather depressing facts about communications between adults and their children as observed in three-minute periods in streets, buses and shops. The researcher, Valerie Yule, watched adult–child pairs in these settings and then compared what occurred with the behaviour of adult pairs. She found that in the time allowed four-fifths of the adult pairs conversed, looked or smiled at each other. By contrast, when adults were accompanying children, during a similar three-minute period, less than half of them had any communication at all with their children; and in two-fifths of the pairs 'what took place was negative'. The children were told off, told to shut up, told to stop what they were doing and hit. Three children crying in pushchairs were smacked. Four children were scolded on buses and smacked. Five children were yanked by arm or hand across a road. One child was cuffed for misbehaving at a bus stop. More than half of the children were ignored whatever they did – whether they cried, played or tried to talk to the adult. The father of a six-week old baby told Valerie Yule, 'We know other parents who smack their babies to keep them quiet. We think that is terrible. All you need to do is shake them.'

Some parents set about punishing undesirable behaviour without paying attention to the needs and 'messages' that lie behind it. Children's communications are often expressed indirectly in a sort of 'code'. This is done unwittingly, since they wish (as all of us do) to be understood. You can be more empathic with your children by attending to what they are saying with an ear tuned to the hidden messages (the 'sub-text'). For example, when children show off in front of strangers they may really be communicating their uncertainty, even (paradoxically) their shyness. I have found it useful, when a child is being a thorough nuisance, making exasperating demands, to say to myself: 'He/she is not trying to be a "problem"; he/she is trying to *solve* a problem. But perhaps the child doesn't have the skill or experience to do it alone. Let me try to find out what it is *really* all about. What is he/she trying to say, trying to achieve?'

An excellent strategy is to *convey understanding* to your child or teenager by bearing in mind the *two-way nature* of good communication between adults. You wouldn't expect another adult to put up with an interminable monologue from you. A true dialogue should also form the basis of conversations with children. A dialogue with a child could sometimes begin with statements indicating understanding rather than reflex statements of advice, criticism or instruction – guaranteed 'conversation-stoppers' with teenagers. Reflective comments provide a mirror of your children's personality; children learn about their emotional likeness (as they get to know their physical likeness) by having their feelings reflected back to them.

The child who comes home saying, 'I hate school', learns that it is not *everything* about school that she dislikes when her mother says 'It's been a bad day today, hasn't it? You have physical education on Monday – are you still feeling a bit embarrassed getting changed in front of the others?' Or when Tom says, 'My teacher made me stay in today', parents would do well to resist the temptation to answer, 'Now what have you done?', or 'I suppose you deserved it', replies which would have inflamed his feelings. Instead, they might acknowledge them by saying, 'You must have felt awful ... would you like to tell me what happened?'

Losing control

Parents who are secure enough to give reasons, to show understanding and to listen carefully know their authority is not threatened by 'giving' a little, by refusing to be 'unbending' at all times. They are also not afraid to 'take charge'. After all, they know more, and have experienced more than their children; they have a legal and moral responsibility to control and care for their offspring.

But there are parents who lose control of their children – most often for reasons that are entirely understandable. The fact is that even infants can influence their upbringing by means of inborn qualities such as temperament. Some are difficult to rear from birth; they 'come on strong', are restless and unpredictable; and their noisy discontent makes parenting seem very unrewarding. Parents can lose their self-confidence (and in such cases it is wise to seek expert help). By their day-to-day actions, children can also affect the way in which their parents react to them in the most powerful and direct manner.

From the time they are born they have the behavioural repertoire to 'shape' their parents' behaviours; and their powers are important for their survival. Some of their repertoire is a sheer delight: they have heart-winning ways – smiles, gurgles and a way of looking at one ... In the technical language of psychologists, they possess a formidable range of 'positive reinforcers' to direct at their parents and others. However, they can also deliver large amounts of what psychologists refer to as 'aversive' (psychologically painful) stimuli if routines are changed or they don't get their own way. As infants they cry or scream, as toddlers they whine or have tantrums, as older children or teenagers they learn to quarrel, argue, sulk and make hurtful remarks. They can also appear miserable, forlorn and even 'heartbroken'. Parents have a wholly understandable desire for their children to be happy, so (not surprisingly) signs of discontent, sadness and storm and stress, are not easy for them to bear. It is difficult to remain calm and objective when one's own child is distressed, even if only through bad temper. The cry of the human infant (and this effect applies especially if it is one's own) is pitched at a level, and varied in such a way, as to be nigh impossible to ignore or get used to. Most adults will go to great lengths (get out of bed repeatedly; stop leaving the child at playschool) to 'switch off' such distressing sounds. Unwittingly *their* behaviour is moulded (i.e. shaped) by the infant's potent demands, and not always in a desirable direction. They suddenly realize that they have become obedient parents and that a tyrannical toddler is effectively 'running' the household. The subject of 'obedient' parents is dealt with at length in chapter 6.

Routines and good habits

You can do a great deal to prevent problems of disobedience and pre-empt countless confrontations if you establish useful routines and personal habits for your child to follow:

Guideline 12: Prepare your child for life by encouraging personal habits and routines.

Most routines are useful short-cuts to living. For example, an adult can dress herself or eat a meal and chat about something else at the same time, because these routines have become automatic habits. Routines help a child to master daily tasks like feeding, washing or going to sleep, so that more can be achieved with less effort. Habit is taught by

Routines and good habits

repetition of routine. A child feels secure if the events of her day are as regular and certain as the sunrise. If going to bed, eating and hairwashing always happen in the same way, she accepts them with little or no fuss.

The bedtime ritual is a particularly powerful habit: a regular routine of supper, bath and then a story before bed makes the child's world seem well ordered, safe and suitable for sleep. Habits of good manners, honesty and consideration for others, which a child acquires by imitating the good examples set by his parents, will stand him in good stead all his life.

Habit, rhythm and regularity are usually helpful to children. They only become annoying, meaningless rituals if they are too rigid or obsessive – when a routine tidying up session turns into a 'you must always put away all your toys and clothes before you get into bed' command, no matter what the unusual circumstances may be that night.

As I have suggested, routines are useful in pre-empting some of the confrontations that arise over getting up, getting washed, getting dressed, getting fed, getting the school bus on time, and so on. These routines, carried out on 'autopilot', help a child undertake daily tasks *around the clock* with *minimum effort or fuss* – once the habits are learned. Giving very young children too much choice over when to get up, what to wear or what they eat for breakfast can be a recipe for disaster – acrimonious arguments, delays and tantrums.

This does not contradict the general guideline that children be given the opportunity to make choices or to discuss reasons. But it does mean giving choices and explaining things to the child at the *appropriate time*. Do avoid long involved debates when you think they are 'delaying tactics' or designed to 'wind you up'.

Chapter Four

How behaviour is learned

As they grow up, children begin to understand that they are separate individuals and see that others have a viewpoint too. Sadly, not all children develop enough sensitivity to other people's values and outlook. They remain self-centred, selfish, disobedient. I shall address the issue of serious (or extreme) defiance later on; for the moment I wish to consider the day-to-day disobedience with which all parents are familiar.

Let us be clear about what we mean by disobedience:

- Your child consistently fails to obey your request (or command) within a reasonable time (say, between five and fifteen seconds, depending on the urgency of the situation). In most cases – and, of course, this is a matter for your judgement of circumstances – allow about ten seconds; *then* you call it 'disobedience'. Of course you may *specify* a time: 'Come away from the edge of the platform *immediately*!', 'Stop pinching your sister, *at once!*', 'Go to bed *when* you finish the chapter you are reading'.
- Your child fails to complete a task you have set, e.g. he fails to eat all his vegetables, she wanders away halfway through picking up her toys.
- Your child (or teenager) fails to keep to the general rules of conduct you have insisted on.

Understanding persistent disobedience

Making sense of persistent and therefore worrying disobedience can be made as simple as ABC. Here is the basic formula:

The principle of reinforcement

Antecedent events are those events that precede, lead up to and set the stage for the disobedient
Behaviour (the disobedient actions), which in turn leads to certain
Consequences – positive or negative – for the child and parent(s).

If you think about and watch the settings of your child's behaviour, it may be that he or she behaves in a non-compliant way, or has a tantrum on some occasions but not others; that is, some situations seem to act as cues for him or her to behave in a particular way. Children tend to tailor their behaviour to the particular places in which, and different persons with whom, they find themselves. This chameleon quality often leads to misunderstandings between home and school – each blaming the other, when more often than not they are difficult in the one setting but not the other. Children tend to look around them, consider the rules, the firmness of the adult, how other children behave and what is expected of them; then they adapt their behaviour accordingly. If your child displays awful behaviour with you, ask yourself: 'Is there anyone to whom she shows her better side?' If so, there may be something worth learning from that person. Antecedents of disobedience are described in greater detail in chapter 6.

The principle of reinforcement

If your child does something you would like her to continue doing – for example, talking to you, asking questions, pointing things out to you, smiling and generally communicating with you – and you take notice, smile, communicate or praise her, she will continue to do it. In technical language, the behaviour has been 'positively reinforced' and thus consolidated. If, on the other hand, you ignore her persistently, then this behaviour is likely to diminish and perhaps even disappear; she will be discouraged. (You will see how we make use of this principle – called 'extinguishing' misbehaviour – for disciplinary purposes later on.) Some parents persistently overlook or ignore their children's good behaviour. However, if your child does something, and as a result of his action something unpleasant happens to him, he is less likely to do it in the future (the undesired behaviour may be reduced or eliminated).

Let us look at some examples. When James asked his brother Nicholas for a turn on his new bike, Nicholas got off and helped James on to the bike – but his mother made no comment, and James rode off without a word of thanks. It would not be surprising if Nicholas didn't share his things next time round. Nicholas's parents also (unwittingly) made bad behaviour worthwhile. When Nicholas was told to leave the television off, he kept putting it on, and eventually it was left on – to give his parents a bit of peace. Again, while Nicholas was having breakfast he kept getting down from his place, and his mother followed him round with a bowl of cereal, feeding him with a spoonful whenever she could. In both of these instances the child's bad behaviour was 're-warded' by allowing him to get his own way. Because Nicholas was rewarded for behaving badly, this behaviour was even more likely to occur again. Parents should ensure that they do not encourage persistent disobedience by rewarding bad behaviour. For example, Jenny wanted to go to the park, but her father said there wasn't time before tea. Although Jenny kicked and shouted, lay on the floor and screamed, her father ignored her tantrum; eventually Jenny calmed down and began to play. Because her behaviour was not reinforced with attention Jenny would be less likely to have a tantrum in the future when refused something.

These examples of patterns of discipline – different parental approaches to good and naughty behaviour – if repeated over and over again in different situations will lead to either a badly behaved (disobedient) child or a reasonably compliant youngster. It really *is* your choice. In order to understand the disciplinary encounters between a parent and child the 'trick' is to examine the positive *and* negative consequences each is applying to the behaviour of the other (see page 110). To change behaviour, we need to alter those consequences. Here, then, is a rule of thumb for your disciplinary efforts:

Acceptable behaviour	+ Reinforcement	= More acceptable behaviour
Acceptable behaviour	+ No reinforcement	= Less acceptable behaviour
Unacceptable behaviour	+ Reinforcement	= More unacceptable behaviour
Unacceptable behaviour	+ No reinforcement	= Less unacceptable behaviour

This discussion of learning provides us with our next guideline:

Guideline 13: Ask yourself *what* your child is doing rather than *why* s/he is doing it.

If you analyse episodes of persistent disobedience in before-and-after sequences, you will gain an understanding of some of the significant influences which trigger and maintain unhappy disciplinary confrontations with your child. By carrying out this exercise you are adopting a constructive approach to your child's difficult behaviour. Rather than labelling it as 'problematic' you are asking yourself: 'What problem is my child trying to solve by behaving in this manner? What does s/he achieve by being so defiant? Is his/her misbehaviour reinforced – wittingly or unwittingly – in the way people respond to him/her? Are there 'payoffs' for behaving badly?'

The evidence tells us that, other things being equal, it is almost certain that children learn faster if they receive *both* positive *and* negative reinforcement. Positive reinforcement tells them what they may and should do; negative reinforcement tells them what they may not and should not do. With both types of reinforcement, children are more fully informed than if they receive only one. Negative reinforcement *does not* necessarily mean the threat of physical punishment. Children may improve their behaviour to avoid disapproval, criticism or the loss of privileges.

A useful guideline is to act rather than talk in times of conflict. Children tend to become 'mother-deaf' at such times. Rudolf Dreikurs maintains that talk is effective only when raised voices imply some impending *action*, and then only momentarily. Usually children know very well what is expected of them. Dreikurs advises parents to restrict talking to friendly conversations and not use it as a disciplinary measure.

The actions to be described next are most effective in the here-and-now; they are designed to resolve *immediate problems*. But they are best followed up later (when the heat is off) with some discussion of what took place. We now have one of the most important of all the disciplinary guidelines in this book:

Guideline 14: Make good behaviour worthwhile.

Strategies for rewarding good behaviour

Praise

The more praise your children receive, the more effort they will make to get more. Always tell them how well they're doing when they try to do up their buttons (even if they can't quite complete the task), put away a toy or own up when they have done something wrong. Symbolic and tangible rewards (praise, encouragement, a hug – the sort of 'rewards' that psychologists call 'positive reinforcers') regulate behaviour. Children are likely to be willing to obey distasteful rules because they wish to have their parents' approval or avoid their disapproval. Words of approbation increase their self-esteem (a theme I shall return to). In this way, they develop patterns of behaviour which conform to the social norm. Not all human behaviours require external reinforcements; children often learn to solve problems simply for the joy of 'doing' or of achievement, which leads to self-reward ('Didn't I do well?').

Incentives

The 'when ... then' rule – sometimes referred to as 'Grandma's rule' – states that 'First you work, then you play' or 'You do what I want you to do before you are allowed to do what *you* want to do'. Clearly this notion, like so many other learning principles, has been known and practised by succeeding generations of child-rearers as simple common sense. However, it has been formally enshrined as the 'Premack principle'.

You might indicate your intentions by saying, for example, '*When* you have fed your dog, *then* you can go out.' An extra incentive can be useful so long as it does not become a too regular (relied upon) habit. If you want your son to leave his paddling pool on a hot afternoon and trot quietly round the supermarket alongside your trolley, then promising to buy ice-cream for tea can be a reasonable bargain. However, the bargain must be made well in advance; it will only undermine your disciplinary strategy if you wait until he is lying on the floor, kicking and screaming and refusing to go to the shops, and then begin promising ice-cream. Then you only encourage him to play up next time and win the ice-cream. So never use rewards or incentives to stop misbehaviour.

When using a rewarding strategy, it is important to make it quite plain to children that they will not be rewarded if they have previously *asked* for a reward ('Mummy, if I do my homework can I stay up late?') and to apply this rule rigorously. Otherwise you might encourage an 'I want ... or else' attitude. A strategy using incentives is best restricted to (and presented as) a way of helping the child learn to do something which is very difficult, or as an appreciation of a special effort (or sacrifice) made. The formula is 'when you ... then I', *not* 'If I ... will you?' With this policy rewards are seen to be under your control – *not* his or hers to manipulate.

You should discuss in advance the reward and the terms for earning it. If you have specified the desired action precisely, there should be no grounds for acrimonious arguments over whether your child has earned the reward or not. Some children do not get enough reinforcement (rewards); others receive far too much without ever earning it. Check on the reinforcers your child receives. Some children are deprived of so few of the 'goodies' in life that it is very difficult to find effective reinforcers – very little is rewarding. However, the opportunity or privilege, to engage in *preferred* activities can reinforce activities or behaviours that are less popular. The value to a child of reinforcing activities can be estimated by observing the frequency of behaviours he or she engages in when completely free to choose (play and TV watching usually figure high on their list of preferred activities).

Some parents worry that rewarding good behaviour is a type of bribery, and believe that a child should do the right thing as a matter of course, simply because it is right. But a bribe is a reward for some corrupt practice. An occasional treat or privilege for a child who has made a big effort to master a new skill or managed to give up a bad habit hardly comes into that category. We all like to award ourselves a little extra something if we give up smoking or lose half a stone, so why not allow the child who is doing something difficult an incentive?

As adults we have active consciences which help us do the right thing. The idea of doing our duty is deeply ingrained in most people, and we tend to forget that children do not come into the world armed with standards of moral and social behaviour. They have to learn the conventions the hard way; small rewards can ease their path. Most of the time they will not need a tangible reward like an extra sweet or a trip to the park. A little praise and an extra cuddle will be enough when the child is young.

Remember that when your child has learned a difficult task it is no longer necessary to give rewards regularly; occasionally you might acknowledge the child's continuing co-operation with a word of thanks or encouragement.

Guideline 15: Accentuate the positive.

Noticing good behaviour

Look actively for the good in your child. Try to catch him or her out in good as well as bad behaviour. It is only too easy to make a 'bad child' out of your offspring by looking diligently for things to criticize. If you want your child to be kind, let him know how pleased you are when he shares sweets or acknowledge her deed when she comforts a younger child who is crying. 'Suggestive praise' as it is called, goes beyond this. You use phrases like 'instead of', 'for not' or 'without', to praise your child for desisting from previous bad behaviour, thus: 'Thank you for sharing your toy *instead of* snatching it away'; 'I think you're a big boy *for not* whining when you couldn't go out'; 'you got ready for bed *without* a fuss'. This method is useful when it is difficult to find positive actions by your child to praise.

Some parents complain that they feel rather awkward going up to their child, when (for example) she is *not* behaving badly, in order to say, 'You *are* painting so nicely, I really feel pleased'. And yet it does pay off. After a bit of practice, 'accentuating the positive' will seem less contrived.

The best and simplest incentives to use are social: taking an interest, praise, smiles, hugs and, for young children, picking them up, smiling, kissing, tickling, rough and tumble – whatever gives them pleasure. Your child really wants your approbation. Always share her success openly and enthusiastically. Never allow one of her triumphant moments to pass without your congratulations. Older children may appreciate a pat on the shoulder or a thumbs-up sign.

What you *say* at such a time is also important. Be specific, don't overdo the praise (flatter), be honest and to the point.

For example:

'I am so pleased *when you do as I ask.*'
'Terrific, I'm so proud of *your result.*'
'Thank you for *doing what I said.*'
'I really enjoy it *when we play quietly* like this.'
'Look at how (nicely, neatly, quickly) *you've done your homework.* I am pleased.'
'I do like *our special time together*' (say reading a bedtime story, chatting to a teenager, playing a game).

I return to the matter of rewarding and how to make it *effective* in chapter 5.

Strategies for ignoring bad behaviour

There are times when it is judicious to turn the 'blind eye' to certain minor infringements (for example, accidents, temporary lapses of memory, impulsive acts that constitute small misdemeanours). The 'Nelson' technique is useful when the child is playing up to force your attention or to 'wind you up'. There is nothing worse for actors than to remove their audience. So, as soon as the misbehaviour begins, turn away or walk away from your child; pretend not to see or hear what is going on; say nothing and try not to show any expression at all; resist getting into any debate, argument or discussion with your child while he or she is misbehaving. If you think your child deserves an explanation for whatever is upsetting her, then say, 'When you have calmed down we will talk about it.'

Guideline 16: Judge when to ignore your child's misbehaviour.

Strategies for ignoring bad behaviour

Ignoring is not the same as doing nothing. This disciplinary technique is designed to ensure that minor misdemeanours such as whining, pestering and tantrums have *no reinforcing consequences*, and it requires a great deal of control and consistency on your part. If a child grabs toys or other goodies from his small brother, make sure the grabbing has no rewarding outcome. Return the toy to its owner but don't get involved in a prolonged argument. You could combine training the older child that grabbing is unproductive with teaching the little one to share, and you should encourage them to take turns. The following is an example of *planned ignoring*:

> Suzy's parents were very concerned at her behaviour during mealtimes when, despite her nine years of age, she would refuse to eat unless fed, would throw food and utensils on the floor and often refuse food entirely. At school lunches she showed none of this nonsense, nor was it displayed at home when she ate informally in front of the television in the evening. Her problem behaviour was specific to family lunch at weekends and holidays, the only occasions when the whole family sat down together at the table. It appeared that this setting was providing Suzy with an audience to which she gladly reacted.
>
> In order to combat this, her parents were instructed to ignore any 'naughty' behaviour and speak to Suzy only when she was eating properly. They were not to feed her or coax her, and any food refused was to be removed without comment. Between meals snacks were forbidden, and the dining room table was arranged so that Suzy's parents were not directly looking at her. Without an audience, but with a very hungry tummy, it wasn't long before Suzy began to eat properly.

Remember that your child may 'work hard' to regain the lost reinforcement and thus may get 'worse' before getting 'better'. You will need to steel yourself for this possible increase (initially) in the behaviour you want to elminate; but don't lose heart – stick to your guns.

Promise yourself before you begin that you will ignore the unwanted behaviour (say, a tantrum) *every* time it occurs, and continue to ignore it until it stops. If you go in and comfort and fuss over your toddler after she has kicked, yelled and 'carried on' for twenty minutes, you will make the situation worse. You have effectively trained her to believe that if she only throws tantrums loudly or long enough she will eventually get a 'payoff' from a relenting (or exhausted) mother or father. You may end up 'training' your child how to escalate her demanding behaviour. For example, you may ignore her persistent whining for attention after one constructive attempt to distract her by suggesting a pleasant and diverting activity (after all, you're having to see to the baby). But then you capitulate when she blows up in a 'force nine' tantrum. If this scenario occurred often enough, you would have taught her that, if whining does not work, a noisy tantrum will do the trick. You have only to give in a few times (out of many when you stick to your planned ignoring) to lose the battle. The occasional or once-in-a-while reward (intermittent reinforcement) will consolidate an established bad habit more effectively than a reward given every time. (The *effective* use of intermittent reinforcement as a rewarding strategy is discussed on page 59.)

Let us look at two examples of these principles applied to two common disciplinary 'problems'. The first – bad language – demonstrates the value of ignoring as a first line of defence. The second – a bedtime problem – illustrates how counter-productive the once-in-a-while reward can be when applied to the wrong behaviour.

Children are fascinated by words they think are 'naughty'. Obscenities have a kind of magic in children's circles and they can be certain of raising shrieks of laughter from their friends, just by saying them aloud. There is extra prestige for

Strategies for ignoring bad behaviour

a child who produces a new word the others do not know. Of course, it is nothing to be alarmed about. Children do hear bad language, not only outside the home but sometimes from parents too. You could even say that you should worry if a child reaches the age of seven or eight without ever using swear words, since he or she may not be listening to people – perhaps not even to you. Children do not have the same need as adults to use bad language to relieve their feelings; they have other ways of letting off steam. But they do enjoy provoking a reaction from adults and being the centre of attention. Overreacting with shock and dismay when the child first comes out with a four-letter word is the best way to ensure he or she uses it again and again. To begin with, ignore any swear words or obscenities the child uses. This may be enough to make him lose interest but, if he persists, discourage him briefly and matter-of-factly, explaining that such words show bad manners and offend some people, who will like him less if he insists on using them. Do not be tempted to tell him that adults are allowed to swear but children are not. One of the attractions of swearing for a child is that it seems a grown-up thing to do. If this method also fails (and do bear in mind that no technique can be guaranteed to work for all children) then try response-cost or time-out (chapter 7).

The once-in-a-while reward is often used to deal with disobedience about coming to the parents' bed in the middle of the night. This is a common problem. For example, the mother of a five-year-old who always cries when bedtime comes may give in every so often and let him stay up late because she cannot bear to see tears. When the same scene happens night after night, his mother realizes that she has been doing the wrong thing, so instead she puts him to bed no matter how long or hard he cries. But the message that bad behaviour no longer brings rewards will take a long time to get through because of its history of being occasionally (i.e. intermittently) reinforced. His mother can speed up the process by putting a star chart on the wall (I discuss these incentives on page 57). At our child and family centre just such a case and strategy led to a 'success story'. However, just as we were all congratulating ourselves, the pattern changed and the child began to come into his mother's bed. Unfortunately, a single lapse in this mother's policy was the first step on the slippery slope of interrupted nights. Her child had a nightmare and she took him into her bed to comfort him. This began to happen regularly. Sometimes, not feeling confident in her judgement that he was playing up, she let him stay. Unwittingly she was operating the *intermittent-*reinforcement principle in support of a bad habit! It is important to appreciate why unforeseen events like these have such long-lasting effects, and to avoid them if you possibly can. You could, of course, go to his/her room to tend to him/her.

I have given two examples of the use of planned ignoring; but it should be borne in mind that ignoring is *not* an all-purpose disciplinary approach. Earlier in the chapter I referred to 'judicious' ignoring; you have to *judge* when it is best to ignore certain childish actions. Ignoring *may* be appropriate:

- when the child has committed a minor infringement (out of forgetfulness, by mistake or in the excitement of the moment);
- when he or she is showing off, throwing tantrums (i.e. playing to the gallery, being self-indulgent);
- when you are feeling compelled to reinforce (reward) inappropriate behaviour by debating/arguing/nagging over it.

General rules are difficult to give because each disciplinary encounter is unique, given the specific circumstances and the individual personalities involved. Ignoring is *not* applicable:

- when the behaviour is potentially dangerous to the child;
- when the behaviour is harmful to others;
- when your child is being downright defiant to you (e.g. saying; 'I won't', 'Do it yourself', etc.).

Chapter Five

Making discipline effective

As I have already emphasized, withholding attention so as not to reinforce undesirable behaviour should be only one part of a dual strategy; the other essential component is a positive and active policy of reinforcing (rewarding) good behaviour. It is of crucial importance to avoid a result in which there is an overall reduction in the quantity or quality of attention given to the child. If you *take away* with one hand, *give* with the other – but at *another*, appropriate time.

If sweet reason and turning a blind eye are not enough and you feel you have to use some form of punishment, do so without excessive anger or physical force. Try to understand that the child is bound to be angry and resentful. He or she should not receive extra punishment for not being overjoyed at being told off. The following pages suggest how disciplinary strategies can be put to the most *effective* use in discouraging unacceptable behaviour and encouraging new and more desirable behaviour.

The importance of timing and consistency

Don't say, 'Wait until dad comes home, then you'll get it!' By then it is too late to be of any good to anyone, and particularly dad.

The importance of the timing of punishment has been effectively illustrated in a series of experiments conducted by Professor J. Aronfreed (an American psychologist) with nine- and ten-year-olds. Toys were shown to the child in pairs, one a particularly attractive and interesting toy, of the kind most children would want to touch, the other with much less appeal. The experimenter instructed each child to pick up and talk about one toy and then applied a mild 'punishment' if he or she chose the more attractive of the pair. The nature and timing of the punishment would vary. Sometimes the child was allowed to pick up a camera (an attractive toy) and then a loud buzzer would sound. At other times the experimenter would take away some sweets the child had previously been given. At yet other times he would say 'No' just as the child was reaching for the attractive toy.

After several trials, the experimenter left the room after putting out a pair of toys. The child was observed through a one-way screen to see whether he or she would resist or give in to temptation (i.e. pick up the more attractive, but forbidden, toy). The degree of resistance to temptation was taken as an indication of the effectiveness of the punishment applied. Children who received punishment *as they reached for the attractive toy* showed greater resistance to temptation than children punished *just after they had picked it up* or at a point *several seconds later*.

> **Guideline 17: Consequences (positive *or* negative) should follow *promptly* the behaviour they are designed to encourage or discourage.**

Another of the experiments demonstrated how important it is, if punishment is to work, for children to understand clearly what they are doing wrong and what alternative actions they can choose. In this study one group of children learned to choose the less attractive of two toys in pairs where the forbidden toy was always of one colour and therefore easy to identify. A second group were shown pairs where there were no colour cues to help them. When an unpleasant sharp sound was used as the 'punishment', the second group, who had the more difficult discrimination to make, learned much less efficiently and became anxious and disorganized.

You can see the parallel in real life to these experiments for those children who are frequently punished for no good reason. Clear rules, fairly and consistently applied, are fundamental to all forms of punishment.

Guideline 18: Try to nip misbehaviour in the bud.

Given the evidence that punishment which immediately *precedes* a forbidden act (rarely possible for busy parents) maximizes resistance to temptation and minimizes guilt, you might try not only to sanction misbehaviour *promptly* but (where possible) forestall your child's action *just as it gets under way*. Don't wait until it has been completed. For example, tap your toddler's hand sharply, with an incisive 'No!', just as he moves to touch the electric fire. Catch her, and check her, as she begins to hurl defiance at you; don't wait for her to complete her tirade.

The possible drawback of this advice is that you may be 'too quick on the trigger' and misinterpret your child's action. So you have the doubly difficult task of being speedy *and* sure of your ground. Here are some supplementary guidelines:

- Make the penalties specific ('You are not going to watch tonight's children's television) not vague ('You wait and see').
- Criticism (like praise) should be related to the particular action that has earned it ('I don't like it when you swear').
- 'The punishment should fit the crime.' The 'tariff' – a loss of privileges, a fine from a teenager's pocket money, a telling off – should be proportionate to the misdemeanour, *not* to the parent's momentary fit of pique or accumulated sense of frustration and resentment.
- The negative consequences of inappropriate behaviour should be predictable to the child: he/she should know what to expect.

This leads on to a major guideline for *all* consequences:

Guideline 19: Be consistent.

When you are teaching children to distinguish between right and wrong and between obedient and disobedient behaviour, you need to be predictable in your reactions. Don't punish them for the way in which they behave today and let them get away with the same thing tomorrow just because your own mood is different, or the matter isn't worth 'all that bother' anyway. If you say no, mean it. Never make idle threats: there's no point in telling a child, 'You won't come shopping with me again if you keep running off' when you know you have to take her along with you.

Of course, there is an element of coercion in discipline. It is no use harbouring romantic, utopian views about this. But it *is* a matter of degree. If your child stays within the limits you set, she has your approval and praise. If she does not, there will be frowns and sharp words and life will not be nearly so pleasant for her. Because she loves you and wants to please you, your disapproval constitutes a real punishment.

Parents often stand out against troublesome behaviour for some time, only to give in eventually. The child asks for something and is told she cannot have it. She goes on pleading and whining, tugging at her father's coat. Finally, exhausted and irritable, he gives in for the sake of peace. The child has learned that if she makes a nuisance of herself for long enough she will be rewarded. If he at last comes to the conclusion that he must stand firm next time, he will need an iron determination, for it will be a long tussle (see page 60).

Perhaps one should ask oneself: what does that moment of weakness – understandable as it might be – that failure to keep my word, have on my child? If (say) the mother is inconsistent, she is, in a sense, only half trying to get her child to behave in the way she desires.

If, for example, a mother has been forced to resort to repetitious shouting, whining appeals and querulous naggings, the child can be said to have learned – learned to 'turn off' what is being said. Eventually he pushes his mother to the point of exasperation where she lashes out at him. Busy parents can justly retort that they have so little time to check on their children, that they cannot always follow through

Balancing punishment with positive encouragement

their threats to discipline them. In the long run, however, the time wasted in nagging exceeds the initial investment in time and effort involved in training children that parents mean what they say.

The major difficulty, of course, is that many parents feel so remorseful after punishing their child, or after losing their temper, that they are sorely tempted to 'make up' to the child, with anything from contrite fussing to extra treats. Children soon take advantage of this inconsistency and the ensuing reward not only negates any potential influence of the punishment (misbehaviour is likely to increase rather than decrease) but debases the currency of the parent's words and deeds.

Balancing punishment with positive encouragement

You won't feel so bad about reprimanding your youngster (indeed, punishing him or her quite severely when the occasion merits it) if you find the appropriate times to display your positive feelings. Punishment will fail if it is not *balanced* by praise, encouragement (and other *positive reactions*) for the sort of behaviours that you are looking for.

The boy who puts unwanted chocolates, sweets, nuts and raisins and chewing gum into the trolley at the checkout *cannot* put his hands to mischief if he is at the other end of the checkout using them to put his mother's groceries in the box (see page 111). She can praise him and give him a little treat. Instead of a tantrum and the ensuing row that prove so reinforcing of defiant behaviour, the mother's words of approval increase the likelihood of future co-operative behaviour. These are good tactics: she is reinforcing actions that *compete* directly with unacceptable behaviours. It takes a bit of imagination and planning – that's all! Even the most Machiavellian child cannot be good and bad *at the same time*.

Unfortunately, many parents tend to be economical in the use of attention or praise for pro-social (as opposed to anti-social) actions – the behaviours they claim to want. Instead, they focus their attention on the negative behaviours they do not want. Teachers have been found to attend to disruptive, inattentive ('off-task') behaviour in their classrooms three times more often than they attend to appropriate behaviour. Parents make statements of praise about their children (e.g. 'well done') infrequently compared with other kinds of comment that are critical. As praise costs so little, this is a regrettable finding to emerge from studies of parent–child relationships. It may therefore be profitable to look further at techniques for strengthening positive actions with positive words and deeds. Children's co-operation can be secured by guiding and helping them towards some desirable action or way of thought. Use a combination of suggestion, appreciation of their difficulties, praise for his efforts and pleasure at their success.

How to encourage (reinforce) effectively

On page 39 I discussed the importance of reinforcers – the incentives that all of us, and not only children, enjoy. You encourage or motivate your child by reinforcing his/her efforts, but this isn't as straightforward as you might think.
First of all, you must make sure you and your child are *clear* about the behaviour you wish to encourage/reinforce. So be specific and precise. Ask yourself, 'What precisely is it I wish my child to say and/or do when I am asking him/her to be good, polite, helpful, kind?' (or any of those other vague goals parents set for their bemused offspring). Here is an example:

Request from child:	'Mum, can I go next door later on?'
Incorrect response:	'Yes, if you're a good boy.'
Correct response:	'Yes, if you stop quarrelling with your sister, and tidy up your toys before you go.'

When the child does what you want, tell him what it is he has done that has earned your praise – for example, 'That was good of you to tidy up your toys. Thank you.' *Be warm and enthusiastic in what you say.* There is no need to make a long speech, though. *Give your praise immediately* after the desired behaviour. Praise every instance when your child is learning something new (e.g. remember to say 'thank you').

Providing cues

In order to teach your child how to act under one set of circumstances but not another, train her to identify the cues that differentiate between the appropriate and inappropriate circumstances. Reward her only when her action is appropriate to the cue – for example, praise her for crossing the pedestrian crossing when the correct signal is given.

Shaping

In order to encourage your child to act in a way in which he has seldom or never before behaved, take your child through mini-steps towards a goal by rewarding any action that approximates the behaviour you want. No reinforcement is given for 'wrong' behaviours. Gradually you make your standards (criteria) of your child's approximations to the correct response more and more stringent until, in the end, he is rewarded only for the precise behaviour that is required.

Artificial incentives or reinforcers: tokens and points

Incentives are considered artificial if the rewarding events would not normally occur as a consequence of the behaviour outside the training situation (e.g. being given stars or happy faces for getting dressed).

Some children who are a real 'handful' do not seem especially motivated by praise and other social rewards. Russell Barkley (an American psychologist, very experienced in helping parents to manage their children) suggests more powerful incentives

Figure 1 *Some suggested reinforcers at home*

Things*	Crayons, plasticene, notepads, play-money, football cards, charms, pencils, marbles, ballpoint pens, comics, records, favourite meals, small toys, book/record tokens, models, puzzles, stamps, magazines, sweets, crisps, fruit, stars.
Activities	Pictures to fill in (in stages), cutting out pictures, drawing/painting, stickers, watching TV, listening to records, playing board games, puzzles, etc., visits, helping mother/father.
Privileges	Staying up late, choice of meal, extra pocket money, extra long story from parent, outing with parent (football match, cinema, etc.).
Social	Kisses, hugs, cuddles (for very young children), pat on the back, words of praise ('great!') and encouragement ('you're doing fine; keep it up').

*The use of 'things', i.e tangible reinforcers, is best applied in cases where there are fairly severe disciplinary problems, or in cases where you wish to reward a special, difficult or sustained effort on the part of your child.

using poker chips (tokens such as counters, buttons, marbles, etc, may be more apt in the UK) for children from four to eight years of age, and a home points system for those of nine and older.

Make a 'bank' with a shoebox or bottle, decorating it suitably. Work out, with your child, a list of privileges the child can earn with tokens (counters) or accumulated points (a notebook is necessary here). On another list itemize the chores or 'good' behaviours you wish to have your child carry out. Work out a tariff: what each task/evidence of good behaviour is worth, in tokens or points. The harder the task, the more the child or teenager earns. Explain the system carefully and do ensure that it is seen to be fair. Give a bonus for a job especially well done.

Russell Barkley suggests, for example, that, for children aged four and five, three tokens are appropriate for jobs like getting dressed without a fuss, clearing up the table, putting away toys, getting ready for and staying in bed. For six- to eight-year-olds he suggests a range of one to ten tokens with larger rewards for big chores or achievements. He recommends that you add up approximately how many tokens you think your child will earn in a typical day if he/she does the little chores you require and behaves in the manner you are trying to encourage. Bearing this number in mind, you decide how many tokens your child will have to pay for a list (something like a menu) of rewards you have constructed, such as choosing a favourite pudding, staying up later than usual, a box of crayons or a special outing. Barkley suggests that children have the opportunity to save a third of the tokens each day to go towards the special rewards on the 'menu'.

A notebook or 'ledger' for older children allows for the depositing of points for good behaviour/tasks fulfilled in the credit column; and the withdrawal of points for misdemeanours or tasks refused, which would be registered in the debit column. The penalty of withdrawal must not be arbitrary: the 'costs' of bad behaviour in the loss of points (see page 74) must be clearly understood by the child or teenager.

You should *phase out* the use of artificial reinforcers (tokens or points) when the child has learned a skill *well*, or when persistent problematic behaviour has been rectified. Ease out the tokens or points on a gradual basis – giving occasional rewards (e.g. more jobs for the same rewards). Warn the child of your intentions. Make use of plentiful social reinforcers and the occasional treat by way of acknowledging your child's continuing efforts.

Being discriminating with rewards

Some children are difficult to motivate because (as I mentioned before) they have been habitually lavished with 'rewards' which have no link to their actions. They don't have to earn or even deserve the praise or the cascade of 'goodies' heaped upon them; consequently they fail to recognize and attribute a causal connection between acceptable behaviour and rewards. Parents in this dilemma might think carefully about being more discriminating with their words of approval and with their reflex action to requests – that of giving and giving and giving.

Expectations are very important. Some children suffer from low self-esteem, and expect to do badly. If a child has a low expectation of passing an arithmetic test, yet is successful, the value of the reinforcement occasioned by the triumph may be great. Failure may motivate the bright and able child yet discourage and handicap the child who is already doing poorly.

Although reward may not represent very much extra incentive for the bright and successful, it motivates the unsuccessful child highly. After all, bright children usually expect to succeed, hence success and praise do not surprise them or necessarily raise them to new levels of performance. If they do not expect to fail or be criticized, when such things do happen, the effect can be powerful. The punishment, as it were, is so severe that they redouble their efforts to avoid encountering it again. However, children who are doing badly tend to expect failure and criticism, since it may have little effect on them except to confirm their worst beliefs about themselves and reduce their efforts. But an experience of praise or reward is so striking and sweet that they work doubly hard to encounter such a state of affairs again.

Parents often ask why they should reward a child for doing something he or she should be doing anyway. The point, of course, is that at the outset the child is *not* doing what he or she should but has to be started off. This is where rewards can prove so useful – as 'starters'. For example, if you wish your 'commanding' child to wait patiently until a more convenient time for her demands to be met, you could reinforce (reward) her for waiting for (say) ten seconds, subsequently you would reinforce her for waiting for a longer interval of time, gradually increasing the interval each time you ask her to wait.

Likewise, if you wish your youngster to persist with a task after he has learned to do it, you should arrange things so that he is no longer rewarded *every time* he gets it right ('continuous reinforcement' is applicable, as we saw, only when the individual is *acquiring* a skill) but only on the odd occasion (a schedule called 'intermittent reinforcement'). This pattern of occasional rewards (something we all experience in daily life) will help your child to maintain a pattern of behaviour *even when you are not there to give encouragement to him.*

Chapter Six

Disobedient children, obedient parents

'She never listens . . . she's a law unto herself!'; 'He seems to think I'm there to obey *his* commands!'; 'She always has to answer back!' This catalogue of complaints represents a group of disciplinary problems that go hand in hand.

Have you ever felt that you (and the family) are in orbit around a controlling, wilful toddler? Have you ever thought, ruefully, that far from raising an obedient child you've become an obedient parent? If so, don't despair: it *is* possible to liberate yourself from this unacceptable 'tyranny' of a toddler (as it so often is) or of an older child. Paradoxically, by taking charge again, you will 'liberate' your child. Children need to feel that their parents are in control; it makes them feel safer. They don't have the experience or wisdom to know best. As I have already noted, I have yet to meet children who were always getting their own way who were contented or calm. Having said that, I do know how overpowering they can be; indeed, I have felt myself withering in the face of a three-year-old's wilfulness.

Of course, all parents (and teachers) are beset at one time or another by disobedient children. But the disobedience I am referring to here is of a very particular kind. Negativism (sometimes called oppositional behaviour) is an exaggerated form of resistance when a child becomes stubborn and 'contrary', often doing quite the opposite of what the mother or father wishes. To put it bluntly, the child goes through a stage of sheer 'bloody mindedness'. This pattern often begins at about eighteen months and reaches a peak between three and six years, after which it rapidly declines. Boys tend to have a resurgence of negativism between ten and eleven years of age.

The reasons why some children and teenagers go 'out of control' or (more accurately) fail to come 'into control' are complex and many.* Some have to do with the child's temperament; others relate to parents' physical and emotional resources and, of course, their methods of discipline (or lack of them!).

It is instructive to observe a parent who is used – perhaps even resigned – to being disobeyed. He or she is likely to be doing one or more of the following when making a request:

- standing well away from the child;
- using a tentative, pleading tone of voice;
- asking a question ('Will you put your toys away for mummy?');
- showing a resigned expression, eyes glazed with the expectation of defeat;
- accepting defeat passively;
- doing the job - say, putting away the toys - for her child.

The fact is that children who are persistently defiant are likely to receive 'payoffs' for being disobedient. They are rewarded

- by escaping from or avoiding unpleasant (boring, difficult, time-consuming) tasks;
- by obtaining a bribe (a sweet to stop the tantrum at the supermarket checkout);
- by 'winding up' their parents;
- by getting the goodies (snatching brother's toy and being allowed to keep it);
- by winning battles of will (feeling big or clever);
- by getting a lot of attention (the fuss, palaver and 'audience reaction' of a tantrum following defiance).

The antecedents of tyrannical behaviour

The ABC formula (see page 39) will help you analyse the antecedents of this behaviour so that you can discover how to

---

* See my *Caring for your Children: A Practical Guide* and *Living with Teenagers.*

The antecedents of tyrannical behaviour

regain control. You need to find out what sets the stage for an act of defiance – what happens before the disobedience, and what are the circumstances in which it occurs.

Rules

To be disobedient, a child has to break a rule. Are the general rules house rules (or 'standing orders')

- clear, i.e. specific and unambiguous?
- understood?
- fair?

Can you put your hand on your heart and say that you have made it plain what he or she *is* allowed to do (hopefully not unnecessarily restrictive) and what he or she should *not* do? If not, sit down and have a chat with your child; but *not* at a time when feelings are running high.

'Disaster areas'

You can predict fairly safely that some of the following situations will be 'disaster areas' for parents:

- getting the child up in the morning;
- washing and getting him/her dressed;
- eating (breakfast and other meals);
- getting the child off to playgroup or school;
- getting the child to obey requests/instructions during the course of the day (e.g. 'Stop teasing your sister', 'Put that chocolate back on the shelf', 'Don't go out on the road');
- defiance of house rules (e.g. breaking rules about playing with matches, about not switching on the TV before the children's programmes begin, about sitting at the table until the meal is finished, or about not taking food out of the fridge without permission);
- interrupting (by pestering) parents when they are in the toilet, on the telephone, cooking a meal, etc.;
- disrupting shopping trips by incessant 'I wants', pulling items off the shelves, tantrums, etc.;

- quarrelling, fighting incessantly with their brothers and/or sisters, teasing, etc.
- not going to bed when asked; not staying there for the night.

Day-to-day requests and commands

Parents with disobedient youngsters tend to 'go wrong' with some of the following points. Do you:

- make *too many commands*?
- use *vague requests* (e.g. 'Why can't you be more polite?' instead of 'Say "please" when you ask for something')?
- *yell out* your commands often from afar?
- *criticize* too many minor points in the child's conduct, making for endless essentially trivial confrontations? (I return to the subject of 'nagging' when I discuss discipline and teenagers.)
- *time* your requests/commands *insensitively*? (Suddenly telling a child to go to bed in the middle of an exciting TV programme is asking for trouble. Warning the child that he or she will go to bed at the end of the programme is much more likely to produce a successful outcome.)
- *let* your child get away with his/her *'misdemeanours'*? Do threats to punish the child remain unfulfilled? Do you allow a stream of orders ('You mustn't!', 'You can't have', 'Stop it . . . or else') to be ignored until 'out of the blue' you lash out with harsh words or actions (perhaps) in order to release your mounting frustration and anger?
- convey 'messages' (wittingly or unwittingly) by the tone of your voice and the sheer volume of criticism and attention paid to the child's bad points that *you dislike him or her*?
- find little time to share enjoyable moments (e.g. play with your children?)

How to regain control

Clear and fair discipline

Remind yourself of guidelines 4 and 5 on pages 14–15 concerning house rules and try to avoid trivializing discipline by unnecessary scolding and nagging (see page 75). If you need to be critical, disapprove of the child's actions, *not* his person. Don't call him names such as 'wicked', 'sly', 'hateful'. Don't threaten her with the police, leaving home yourself or sending her away. Always try to be incisive. Take charge! Show the child you mean what you say by making use of businesslike but courteous commands and instructions.

Identifying trouble spots

Alert yourself to the most likely 'trouble spots' in your life (when it comes to discipline) by filling in the questionnaire or a photocopy of it (see figure 2). Forewarned is forearmed! I will be providing some advice (later on) about how to manage some of these situations.

Figure 2   *'Trouble spots' questionnaire*

My child is disobedient:

	Often	Seldom	Never	It amounts to a real problem for me
At home				Yes/No
Visiting				Yes/No
Shopping (or other public places)				Yes/No
At playschool or school				Yes/No
When out playing				Yes/No

My child gives me trouble:

	Often	Seldom	Never
When getting ready (e.g. dressed) in the morning.			
At mealtimes			
When going to bed			
Over staying in bed			
Over watching TV			
During washing/bathing			
When I'm occupied (on the phone/talking to someone/in the toilet)			
When asked to do something			
When asked to stop doing something			
Over keeping to the general rules			
Doing homework			
In the car/bus			

How to give clear commands

In order to make effective requests and commands, you might try the following steps recommended by the Australian psychologist Alan Hudson:

- Use the child's name.
- Give a *specific* direction.
- Include a mention of time (e.g. 'right now' or 'when you have finished the chapter').
- Say 'please'.
- Get all the words together (in the form of a statement, *not* a question). Do not say: 'Sandy, will you get dressed for mummy?' Do say: 'Sandy, I would like you to get dressed now, please.'
- Make the request standing *close* to the child; with a young child get down close to the height of the little one.
- Use a pleasant but *firm* tone of voice (no pleading, cajoling, wheedling!).
- Try to be looking at the child when you make your request. It may be helpful to say, 'Sandy, look at me now, please', and then give the desired command. (With an inattentive, hyperactive child you might hold him in front of you and ask him to repeat your request as a check that he has 'taken it in'.)

Guideline 20: Make your requests/demands in a clear, firm and confident manner.

If the child obeys within (say) ten seconds, follow the behaviour with clear and predictable consequences; do likewise if he/she disobeys by refusing or ignoring you over that time period. Obedience is followed by positive consequences (e.g. the acknowledgement of a 'thank you' or praise); disobedience is followed by negative consequences (e.g. loss of privileges, time-out (see page 70).

How to regain control

Changing the consequences

The important matter of consequences (rewards, penalties and punishments) can be illustrated with an example from the home setting.

Andrew was a toddler when I met him; he was an expert at tantrums when he didn't get his own way. I advised his parents to make their son's temper tantrums unrewarding (indeed *costly*) while *at the same time* making co-operative behaviour highly beneficial to him. This is how I put it:

> Andrew has not yet learned to control his temper. He 'lets go' in a frightening tantrum – banging his head, kicking, screaming and yelling – when he cannot get his own way, such as when you try to insist on his doing something, refuse his commands or attend to people other than himself at a time when he wants your undivided attention. The consequence (usually) is that he achieves his goal; he coerces you both into giving way – a very rewarding state of affairs seen from his point of view, a very unrewarding (and sometimes humiliating) state of affairs seen from your perspective. Occasionally you stick to your guns which means that Andrew has been getting rather inconsistent messages: he can't anticipate the consequences of *his* undesirable actions since *your* reactions are not predictable. Sometimes (but rarely) you punish his unacceptable behaviour, generally when there are visitors. Sometimes you ignore it, for example, at the supermarket. Generally you 'reward' it and thus make it more likely to recur, by giving in to him. Andrew has learned to make this outcome more likely by escalating the tantrums into very violent and therefore frightening episodes.
>
> We now have to alter the old *consequences* and make it quite clear to him that his bad behaviour will have results that are not only not rewarding, but also unpleasant enough to make him relinquish his tantrum. You have tried smacking, which you admit makes him worse and you miserable. You will use a method called response-

cost – in essence, fining his tantrums (see page 74). But at the same time you will make it very beneficial for him to be more obedient, to ask nicely and to control his temper. We will record his successes on this star chart and show him how he can earn treats when he has collected a specified number of stars [see page 57].

Consequences in the form of penalties and punishments are the subject of the next chapter.

Chapter Seven

Penalties and punishments

There are many people who believe sincerely that you can train children for life without resorting to punishment. If they equate punishment with physical punishment, I can see their point and would generally agree with them (although most parents would feel that such a proposition is very difficult to apply). If they are equating punishment with the wider range of non-physical penalties, however, I would not agree (for reasons I will explain later). It is important to review all these methods as they figure so strongly in the consciousness of people when they think of discipline.

Guideline 21: Tell children what they should do, as well as what they can't do.

I have been at pains to emphasize the *positive* aspects of discipline. Positive consequences (social rewards such as praise) show the child what he or she *should* do. Punishments – or penalties, as I prefer to call them, because of the association of the word 'punishment' with physical retribution – show the child what he or she *shouldn't* do. In fact, positive consequences are not always enough when used alone. You will, at times, have to make the consequences of undesirable behaviour *costly* for the child.

Ignoring is regarded by the child as a punishment, even if you don't see it like that. In chapter 4 I suggested that you might try ignoring certain categories of unacceptable behaviour. I can well imagine that you were protesting that there are behaviours (like aggression) which you simply cannot ignore. Of course this is so. And that is where time-out may prove useful – especially in tense, angry situations. It also comes in handy in cases of defiance when the child digs its heels in and says 'No!' or 'Won't!' Ignoring is counter-productive in such confrontations.

Time-out

The 'time-out' procedure is intended to reduce the frequency of an undesirable behaviour by denying the child any opportunity to acquire reinforcement (for example, getting everyone stirred up, getting his/her own way, becoming the centre of attention) as a result of his or her misbehaviour. You have possibly used a version of this method. There are three forms of time-out:

- *Activity time-out*: the child is simply barred from joining in an enjoyable activity, but still allowed to observe it – for example, having disrupted a board game, she is made to sit out of the game.
- *Room time-out*: the child is removed from an enjoyable activity, not allowed to observe this, but not totally isolated – for example, standing at the far end of the sitting room, or sitting on a straight-backed chair.
- *Seclusion time-out*: the child is socially isolated in the hall or another room. (If your child tries to come out prematurely, hold the door shut but *don't* argue or hold a conversation with him.).

If time-out didn't work for you, you may have been applying the method incorrectly. It requires great care and its use must be *precise*, *consistent* and *persistent*. Research has shown the method to be by far the most effective disciplinary technique to use in situations of defiance and (as often occurs) the ensuing aggression.

The correct way of using time-out is as follows, (see also figure 3). The child is warned in advance about those behaviours that are considered inappropriate and the consequences that will follow from them. Time-out may last for five minutes (no more). Two or three minutes are sufficient for pre-school children.

As an example, let us imagine that you have made your request/command in the manner described on page 66. Count to ten (but *not* aloud). If your child has not made a move or defiantly says, 'No, I won't', repeat the command in a louder voice. If he/she fails to comply promptly, say, 'If you do not do as I asked you *immediately* you will have to sit on the chair in the hall.' (A chair at the other end of the room or isolation in a *safe, unstimulating (unfrightening)* room elsewhere in the house are your other options. It is preferable not to use your child's bedroom, since you don't wish to associate it with punishment.) Do not become strident; it is critical that you appear calm *and* in control (however stirred up you may feel inside). Again count silently to ten. If you are still being defied take the child by the wrist to the chair in the hall. Make *no* comment as you go. (Arguments, debates or discussions about the 'rights and wrongs' of the punishment would be wholly counter-productive!) Before leaving the child in time-out say: 'You stay here until I tell you.' Time the (say) three minutes. On your return, ask your child quietly: 'Are you ready to do as I asked?' This would be your line in the case of defiance. In the case of aggression (pinching, swearing, tantrums, etc.) ask the question: 'Do you agree not to do that again?'

After your child has complied and performed the request (say, picking up his/her toys) but *not* before, say quietly, 'I *am* pleased when you do as I ask.' Look out for the next genuine opportunity to praise your child for some acceptable behaviour. If the child does not comply you may have to repeat the three-minute interval several times. Do persevere!

If you are consistent and timely in your application of time-out, it shouldn't be long before the word 'time-out', in the form of a warning question (plus a look or gesture), is sufficient to quell a defiant or aggressive action.

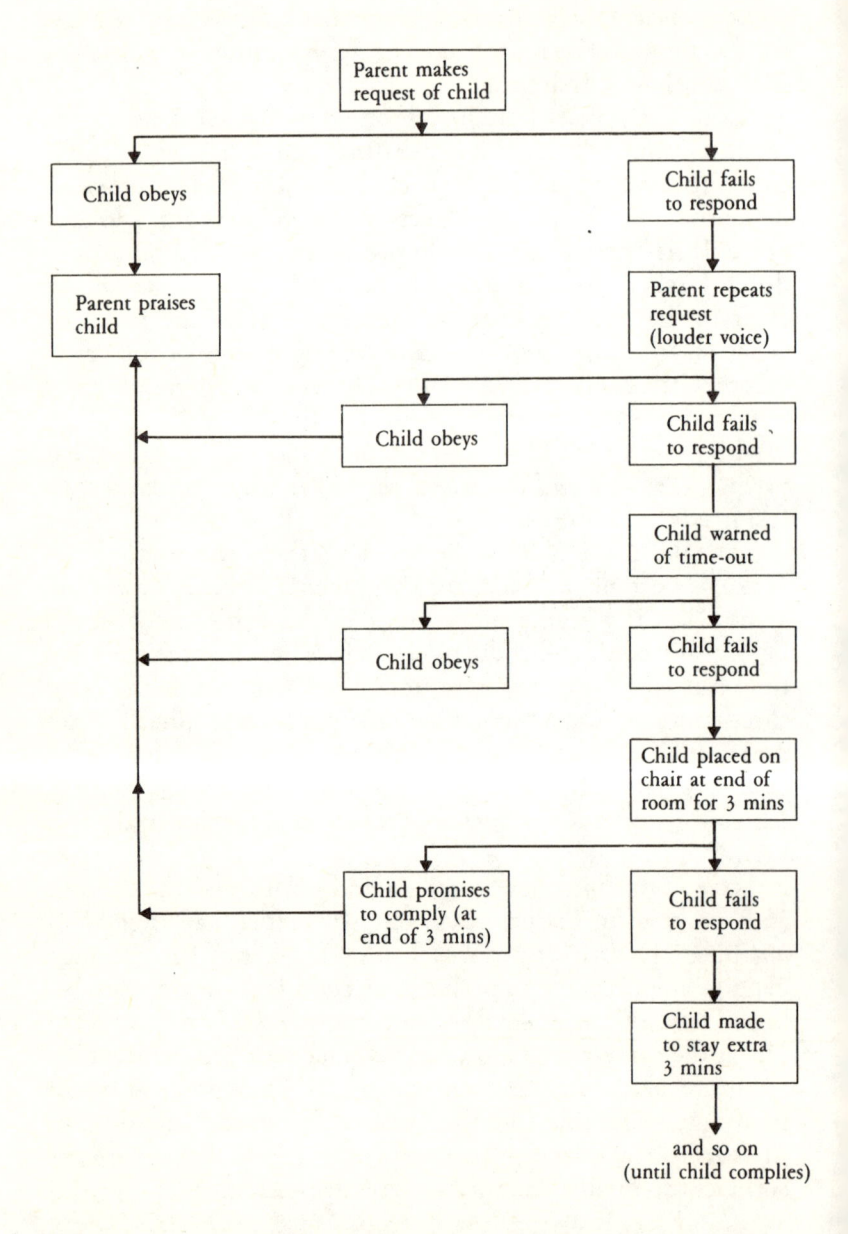

Figure 3 *An example of the stages in the use of time-out*

Time-out

The following points should be borne in mind:

- Activity or 'room' time-out is always preferable, where feasible, to any form of 'seclusion' time-out.
- Time-out is unlikely to succeed unless it is part of a *dual* strategy in which you supplement the method with rewards for alternative, appropriate ways of behaving.
- The more 'costly' your child finds it to be removed from the limelight or from whatever he/she finds rewarding about misbehaving, the more effective is time-out likely to be. (This is why time-out should be as boring as possible – it then becomes a real penalty.)
- Don't make a fuss when the child comes out of time-out.
- Time-out if administered firmly, insistently but gently, usually results in the child's going to the chair or the hall like a lamb. But it does provoke rebellious, aggressive behaviour in a minority of children, particularly if they have to be taken by force to a quiet room, or the door has to be held to keep them there. You are the best judge of when this approach is counter-productive. With older, physically strong, resistive children, time-out may simply not be feasible. You may then need to consider response-cost (described below).
- When time-out is difficult to administer because the child is strong, the parent (i.e. a major source of reinforcement) could remove herself (together with a magazine) to the bathroom - coming out only when all is quiet.
- When you are away from home, try to think up some novel way of isolating your child temporarily from ongoing activities (see page 84).

Preventing a young and disruptive child from playing, but allowing him/her to watch the others at play, may also do the trick. This method – removing an aggressive nursery school child from play for a period of one minute – was compared by researchers with a scolding and orders not to hit and with a further method of distracting (i.e. redirecting) him to other play. The removal-from-play technique was much more effective than scolding or distraction at reducing aggressive episodes.

Response-cost (fining)

Response-cost procedures involve the forfeiture of rewards or privileges currently available – such as going out to play or staying up late on Friday evening. The failure to complete homework for example, results in the loss of television-viewing time.

To stop a child from acting in an unacceptable manner, you should arrange for him or her to terminate a mildly unpleasant situation immediately by changing the behaviour in the desired direction. For example, every time he or she throws a toy in a dangerous manner the offending toy is locked away.

If your child does something you do not like, such as losing her temper too easily, you may *increase* her ability to think first and hold her temper by penalizing her consistently for failing to do so; in this way you are providing an 'incentive' for her efforts to keep her cool. For instance, if you say, 'Donna, if you do not think first, but lash out at your sister, I will not allow you to go to the fairground with me', her resolve to think first and desist from hitting out will be strengthened. She can avoid punishment by appropriate actions. The parents may not have to apply the penalty if she believes their threat because of their record of keeping their word. *Consistency* and *persistence* are watchwords in early learning, especially with certain volatile (hyperactive) children who find it difficult to concentrate for long enough to absorb life's lessons.

The general principle on which response-cost is based, is referred to by psychologists as *negative reinforcement*. Behaving in a manner that *avoids* an unpleasant outcome leads to the reinforcement of behaviour you wish to encourage, thus making it more likely to recur in similar circumstances. Negative-reinforcement techniques give parents (and teachers) three training methods. In a sense you are saying one of the following:

- 'If you do the desirable thing I will withdraw a penalty.'
- 'If you don't do the desirable thing I will present a penalty.'
- 'If you don't do the desirable thing I will withdraw a reward.'

Reprimands (criticizing/shouting)

The withdrawal of privileges is a very popular response by parents to non-compliance – for example: 'You've been cheeky so I won't let you go out'; 'You disobeyed me by going out on the road so you can't have that ice-cream.' When you warn your child that you will withdraw a privilege if he or she does X, Y or Z, make sure it is a threat that you can deliver. If you say, 'I won't let you go to any parties' or 'You can't go out to play for a week' you will probably reconsider when you cool down, change your mind and thus lose credibility. So don't make the fines/costs too high. Keep them in proportion to the action being penalized.

Overcorrection

Teaching children to make reparation is an important lesson in life; overcorrection takes this one stage further. The child must not only remedy the situation caused by his or her negligence or transgression but also 'overcorrect' it to an improved or better-than-usual state. In other words, you enforce the performance of a new behaviour in the situation where you want it to become routine. Get the child to practise positive behaviours which are physically incompatible with the inappropriate behaviour.

For example, a child who steals and breaks another youngster's penknife is required to save up enough money not only to replace the knife, but also to buy a small gift betokening regret. She is praised at the completion of the act of restitution. A boy who deliberately punctures another child's bicycle tyre not only has to repair the tyre, but also must oil and polish the entire vehicle.

Reprimands (criticizing/shouting)

A 'telling-off', be it at maximum decibels, or in a quiet but cutting tone of voice, is probably the most frequently used form of sanction. We know that the parents of aggressive children use more ridicule, nagging and scolding than other parents. There is evidence that verbal reprimands tend to be less effective in various disciplinary encounters than other techniques. However, just as there are degrees of physical punishment (see pages 77–8), there are variations in verbal punishment. Although insistent scolding, nagging and criticizing may be counter-productive, the effects of a really loud, convincing 'No!' – the kind of short, sharp verbal 'shock' which a mother can produce when she sees her child about to poke her finger into her baby brother's eye – may well be highly successful.

Physical punishment

In the minds of many people the word 'punishment' is equated with physical punishment: smacking, caning, slapping and the like. Not surprisingly those parents who are against physical punishment in principle are quite likely to assert that they never punish their offspring. Yet it is a fact that even the most permissive of mothers and fathers intentionally or unwittingly punish their children in the course of socializing them. It has been put in this way by the psychologist Richard Walters:

> Many permissive parents who would never dream of beating or otherwise hurting their child may frequently utter a harsh word or send the child from the room for misbehaving. Such actions may cut as deep or more deeply than all but the most violent of thrashings. In no sense are shouting and isolation punishers necessarily secondary to more 'fundamental' pain-producing stimuli. Although a number of theorists have defined punishment as a 'pain-producing stimulus' the majority of apparent punishments experienced in everyday life are not, strictly speaking, painful.

Walters observes: 'unfortunately, it is so often the case that it is the painful, extreme, and perhaps rare effects of punishment that are stressed while the "thorns and little shocks" that occur day in and day out which may ceaselessly, slowly and effectively change our habits and, indeed, our destinies are ignored.' Some parents, for example, specialize in threats, notably the counter-productive and fear-provoking ones involving policemen, monsters and kidnappers who will harm or remove the child if he or she doesn't comply.

Most parents smack their children sometimes. In a famous study by John and Elizabeth Newson in Nottingham, *Four Years Old in an Urban Community* (1970), the figure was 97 per cent. Half of these mothers said they smacked only in anger; the remainder used smacking deliberately as a disciplinary technique. For all its 'popularity', many parents feel a sense of guilt when they smack. They also wish to know whether punishment – be it physical or psychological – is of any use whatsoever.

What does one say to the mother who complains that sometimes her child will go on and on doing something that is not only naughty but dangerous. Distracting him doesn't work; talking to him nicely doesn't work; in the end, only a slap on the leg cuts through all the tension and nagging. And she adds, 'Sometimes I even get the feeling that he's deliberately working up to a smack; almost testing me out, pushing me to the limit!' What is the harm if she is driven occasionally to let go with a smack? It is very doubtful whether the occasional smack meted out against a background of a loving, accepting home, does anyone much harm; but this is true only if the punishment is not too severe or excessive.

There is general consensus in the research studies that physical punishment does 'work' in the limited sense that it will *suppress* many behaviours quickly and completely – the latter *only if* alternative (competing) and desirable behaviours are encouraged with positive reinforcement (rewards).

Most physical punishments used by parents are not intended to be, or experienced as, particularly painful. They represent, generally speaking, signals of warning (like the nips and cuffs of the protective mother bear) or symbols of displeasure. In this sense they are part of a system of communication between parent and child. They usually emerge at the end of a chain of exasperating events – a toing-and-froing between parent and child – and convey an unambiguous parental message: 'I have had it! Enough's enough.'

'Smacking' or 'spanking' are, of course, euphemisms. They refer to a carefully measured and controlled response to provocation. It doesn't sound quite so *physical* as a 'whipping' or a 'hiding'. And certainly the smacks administered by most human mothers are a type of 'short, sharp shock' constituting a mild form of aversive conditioning.

For critics of corporal punishment such a rationalization (as doubtless they would see it) is not good enough. They believe that the link between a permissive attitude towards corporal punishment and child abuse is a distinct possibility and that there should be laws to forbid any adult from striking any child, including their own. Children are people, not property, they argue; and if it is wrong to hit people then it must also be wrong to hit children.

Unfortunately, smacking tends to be habit-forming; there are parents who lack judgement and self-control; and some do not appreciate that a blow to the child's head and other parts of the body, even a severe shaking, can be downright dangerous – sometimes fatal. Some parents make regular use of extreme force. Yet, if there is one principle that has been established by scientific investigation time and again, it is that *physical violence* is the least effective form of negative reinforcement when it comes to *moulding a child's behaviour*. All the evidence to date – and there is a considerable body of it by now – shows that physical methods of punishment (the deliberate infliction of pain on the child) may for the time being suppress the behaviour that it is meant to inhibit but will not form character.

Violence (and I am deliberately using a word that denotes severe aggression) begets violence. What the child learns is that might is right. Delinquents have more commonly been the victims of adult assaults – often of a vicious, persistent and even calculated nature – than non-delinquents. Boys who were caned at school for smoking were found to be more likely to increase their smoking than those not caned.

Allan Fromme, a clinical psychologist and therapist, gives

his reasons for believing that persistent, excessive punishment is a policy of defeatism:

> You are teaching him to fear and hate you when you spank him.
> You are building up his arbitrary obedience to conscience instead of his understanding and acceptance of ethical standards.
> In expressing as much bad temper as he does, you are offering a bad example for him to imitate.
> There is less skill and ingenuity in the use of brute force than any other technique.
> Spanking may actually stamp in, rather than eliminate, your child's misbehaviour.
> The goal of discipline is to modify *desire*, not merely behaviour.

Dr Benjamin Spock points out, however, that if an angry mother refrains from spanking she may show her irritation in other ways, for instance, by nagging the child for half the day or trying to make him feel deeply guilty. Spock is not advocating spanking, but he thinks it is less destructive than lengthy disapproval, because it clears the air for both parent and child. This is how he qualifies his advice:

> The right punishment is the one which seems right to the parent and which works. It all depends on the parent, on the child, and on the misbehaviour.
> A slap on the hand or the behind works like a charm for one parent–child combination. Another mother only feels like a brute for hours afterwards; and another child is made furiously resentful by this indignity. A brief isolation in his room sweetens up one child in five minutes. Another child makes the family wretched with his crying for the better part of an hour. Fines and withdrawal of privileges are more appropriate for the school-aged child, and when they are fair and not run into the ground they even appeal to his sense of justice.

In another case, though, they lose all moral value and lead only to bookkeeping and arguing.

So there is no system of punishment that is neat or that will work the same in any two families or that will function automatically.

Punishment *alone* has never made a bad character into a good one, or even ensured temporary good behaviour.

Good discipline is mainly based on mutual love and respect. In childhood it has to be reinforced with teaching, firmness, reminders. Punishment is only one form of reminder, a particularly vigorous one for emergencies - usually with strong feelings involved - to get a child back into the groove.

To sum up:

- The background to physical punishment is what is all-important. Punitive methods *persistently* used against a background of rejecting, hostile parental attitudes lead, in the long term, to trouble. The occasional smack meted out in a happy, secure home is not going to scar a child's psyche.
- The real trouble with smacking is that it is too easy. It doesn't require much thought, and in the *short term* it works. A smack terminates the child's naughty behaviour, thus bringing relief to the harassed parent. This reinforces the likelihood that he or she will smack the child again in similar circumstances, so that it tends to become a way of life. (However, this particular aspect of child-rearing is one in which it is only too easy to pontificate from the ivory tower – introducing idealistic values and utopian solutions which the busy parent with several young children must find somewhat ironic.)
- A smack may suppress unwanted behaviour but it won't indicate alternative actions to children – the things they *should* do.
- In some emergencies, as when a young child tends (despite previous explanations and warnings) to rush out into the street, the point made above is not a matter of primary concern. The parents' aim is straightforward: to get the

child to desist from potentially dangerous behaviour, not to teach alternatives.
- If parents want their child to learn how to be co-operative, honest, reliable (or other desirable things), smacking will not help. It may, in fact, be counter-productive because it produces a state of high emotional arousal (anger or anxiety) that is notorious for interfering with the acquisition of new skills and behaviours.

Perhaps smacking should be regarded as a last resort and even then as something of a failure in communication between parent and child. Children who are able to understand explanations and who enjoy a relationship of trust and affection with their parents usually listen to *firm* demands and prohibitions from them – especially if they know why they are necessary. One mother has observed:

> I don't spank my children. I can't recall really spanking them. I have had occasion where, when I have wanted – felt the urge – to strike, and oh, sometimes when I've seen her temper and Jill is stamping around, and I'll say, 'All right, upstairs you go.' And if she doesn't go right away, I'll just give her a little motion on her rear and that's about all. But you wouldn't call that a spanking. That's, well, it kind of lets my steam off a bit; it doesn't hurt, but she knows I mean business. And she doesn't recognize it through the pat on her bottom; she recognizes it in my tone.

Natural and logical consequences

Life itself, and its sometimes harsh realities, provides penalties which teach individuals about the 'costliness' of their misdemeanours. Rudolf Dreikurs suggests that parents might use life's natural consequences – the reality of the situation – rather than parental power to deal with misbehaviour. For example, when a child is playing so destructively with a toy that it is likely to break, if the *natural consequence* occurs and the toy breaks, the child is able to learn from the outcome of his/her actions. Experience is what we learn from our mistakes. But some parents don't allow their children to experience the consequence of their actions. Parents are (understandably) likely to protect their child. They let them 'off the hook' by, in a sense, putting *themselves* on it. In the long run they will have to bear the consequences of an unrealistic and immature child.

A *logical consequence* occurs when the parent intervenes and (in the example above) *removes the toy* while indicating that the child has 'chosen' or decided to play without the toy for a specified period of time because of his or her actions (it is a form of response-cost). A child *must* be old enough to understand what the natural consequences of his or her actions are likely to be. For the older child one warning of your intention to use this method would seem only to be fair.

The consequences of a child's actions might be as follows:

- The child won't get out of bed when his mother calls him in the morning: so he misses the school bus, is late for school and is punished by his headteacher.
- The teenager won't put her soiled clothing in the laundry basket as requested; they don't get washed. Eventually the day comes when the party clothes (the 'specials') aren't there for her to wear.

It is important to remember that logical consequences are never to be used as an idle threat. Should you say, 'Unless you stop quarrelling with your sister I won't be able to finish my work and there won't be time for a story', you must be prepared to see through the planned, but logical, consequences. Don't give in to tears and special pleadings. Grit your teeth and hold back. The natural consequences of a child's misbehaviour (if not forestalled or prevented) might be far from his or her liking. *If* you can allow your child or your teenager to experience these consequences (short of any which might cause them serious pain or hurt), he or she will learn from them without the addition of sermons, scolding or smackings. Experience of reality provides the salutory lesson. So don't put yourself out *unless* the implications or consequences of your child's behaviour are harmful, irreversible or, in some other way, serious.

Combining methods

Penalties may be combined with rewards in order to modify children's behaviour. I mentioned some 'disaster areas' in chapter 6. Many of these are situations where it is difficult (or embarrassing) to apply your disciplinary skills. Your child knows, or thinks, she has put you at a disadvantage by her highy cunning tactics: you are made vulnerable by her highly visible (indeed, audible) tantrums and disobedience in public places, whether in supermarkets, on public transport, at the park, during a church service or a visit to the doctor. In such situations you might combine the methods we have discussed, in a manner suggested by a psychologist, Michael Griffin, to cover these situations.

- Prepare your child for each visit by explaining how you want her to behave. If you are shopping, stop outside the shop and go over the rules and consequences. Indicate precisely which behaviours are unacceptable. Where possible give her some task to carry out during the outing, for example, helping to find the items on a shopping list. If possible, help your child to practise the correct behaviours while still at home.
- Carry a 'black book' on outings, and record in it unacceptable behaviours by writing a short description in front of your child (such as 'wandered off in supermarket'). Warn your child first that you will record the behaviour in the black book if it doesn't stop immediately. Also *praise your child for acceptable behaviour* and record this in the book on a separate page (such as 'helped carry shopping'). When you return home, you can convert the good and bad behaviours noted in the book into tokens or points won or

lost (see page 58). The 'costs' may lead to the loss of, say, television-watching time (see response-cost on page 74).
- Quite often, rewards and penalties can be applied on the spot. For example, you could reward a child for staying with you in the supermarket by buying a small treat as you leave. State the condition before you begin shopping: 'You can have a comic if you stay close by me while I am shopping.' Penalties can also sometimes be applied on the spot, for example, by removing your child to your car for five minutes, while you remain outside it (don't leave your child in a car unless you are close). If travelling in a car, you might stop for a few minutes as a penalty, refusing to speak to the child until he behaves.

The following case shows how a penalty such as time-out can be combined with positive reinforcement of pro-social behaviour.

> Gary was six and a half years old at referral and was described as a very unlovable child. He constantly screamed and shouted abuse at his parents and had violent temper tantrums when he would indulge in physical aggression, hitting and punching people and furniture, and screaming at the top of his voice until he got his own way. He was also persistently defiant and disobedient and seemed to enjoy provoking confrontations with his parents. Observation and assessment confirmed that Gary was indeed showing all these behaviours, but also revealed that they were being heavily reinforced by attention from his parents and by the fact that the shouting and temper tantrums usually resulted in Gary's getting his own way.
>
> Not surprisingly, against this background, family relationships were very strained and Gary was so unpopular that on the rare occasions when he did behave appropriately it went unnoticed and unattended to, which meant he was only getting attention for antisocial behaviour.
>
> To deal with the shouting and temper tantrums

associated with disobedience, his parents removed Gary from the room as soon as he started to shout. His release from time-out required that he quieten down and comply with the original request on his return. The parents were able to eliminate the intimidating outbursts almost entirely. At the same time great emphasis was placed on rewarding Gary for pro-social behaviour – obedience, co-operation – with tokens which he could then exchange for a privilege (such as staying up late) or a treat (such as a favourite play activity with his parents).

This programme was designed to improve their relationship with Gary by providing opportunities for mutually reinforcing activities. By the end of the programme Gary was much happier, showing much more pro-social behaviour and getting on a good deal better with his parents.

This case illustrates how by changing behaviour one can also affect attitudes. By modifying children's more difficult behaviour, they become more rewarding to their parents, and mothers and fathers who have been at the stage of rejecting and even abusing their difficult children find they can enjoy the experience of being a parent.

Chapter Eight

Understanding anger and aggression

Forms of anger and aggression

Children give vent to their anger in various ways. They may attack others physically or verbally, screaming all the insults they can invent; or they may be destructive, wilfully damaging or destroying anything that is handy when they lose their temper. Many go through a phase of biting, hitting or even bullying other children (especially younger siblings). Fortunately parents *can* do a lot to tone down the aggressive behaviour. Hitting the child harder so that 'he will see what it's like' will probably only increase his anger and need for vengeance – besides teaching him that if you are bigger and stronger, you can always win.

Fighting and feuding

If you see your small child trying to hurt a playmate, pull her away firmly without slapping and find something else to interest her. If she tends to dominate children of her own age and push them round, try to arrange for her to play with older children who will have no trouble in holding their own.

It is not so easy to change the playmates when they are brothers and/or sisters (siblings), and many parents tell me of their concern about the seemingly incessant feuding that goes on among brothers and sisters. Parents love each child, and it grieves them to witness the hitting, hurting and hateful things said to each other. Far too much time and energy go into separating combatants, settling differences and trying to encourage children to get on together. It has all the joy of being in a United Nations peace-keeping force. Eventually, most youngsters outgrow the jealousy and bickering, and begin to feel affection and care for each other. This is a sign of dawning maturity. Others continue the hostility into adulthood and never make peace with their brothers and sisters – a phenomenon called sibling rivalry.

When I talk to parents I find that they have tried most known procedures for stopping fights – but still the squabbles continue. Quarrelling among siblings is so common that it has become accepted as 'normal'. But feuding and fighting are not acceptable just because they occur so frequently. Children do not have to fight; homes where children do not quarrel endlessly are possible. When children quarrel excessively, there is something going badly wrong with their interactions and relationships, since few of us really enjoy arguing and fighting.

Anger and quarrels

Anger is an emotion all children experience. Very young babies show rage, turning scarlet in the face and screaming, but only when they become toddlers can they hit out at whoever is preventing them from doing what they want. As the child gets older, the undirected or unfocused displays of emotional excitement (crying or screaming) become more rare, and aggression that is retaliatory more frequent. It is not easy for young children to learn to 'wait patiently', 'ask nicely', and to be generous, considerate and self-sacrificing. They try to get their way by fighting for it.

The social interactions of young children (not least those with siblings) are marked by aggressive, conflict-ridden behaviour. Anger, hostility, quarrelling and combativeness (as parents and teachers can testify) are frequently to be seen in children's relations with each other. A psychologist, Professor H. C. Dawe, investigated the quarrels of pre-school

American children during the morning free-play period at nursery school. Forty boys and girls (25–60 months of age) were observed and a total of 200 quarrels were analysed. She found that:

- The average duration of the quarrels was 23 seconds – surprisingly short. Quarrels among the older children lasted longer than those among the younger.
- Boys quarrelled more frequently and were more aggressive during quarrels than girls.
- Quarrelsomeness tended to decrease as children got older.
- The youngest children started the most quarrels but took the less aggressive role during the quarrel. As children grew older aggressiveness and retaliation increased.
- Children quarrelled most often with those of the same sex.
- The majority of quarrels were started by a struggle for possessions. The number of quarrels of this type decreased with age but still held the lead over other types for all ages.
- Pushing, striking and pulling were the most common activities. The older children indulged in the more violent forms more often.
- Crying, forbidding and commanding were the most common forms of vocal activity, although silence was a more frequent reaction than any other.
- Talking during a quarrel increased with age, but dialogues were rare.
- Quarrels of the argumentative type increased with age.
- The average number of quarrels per hour was three to four, although this was probably an underestimation. There seemed to be more quarrels indoors when the children were crowded together.
- The children settled the majority of the quarrels themselves, most frequently by one child's forcing another to yield. Most often the younger child was forced to yield to the older, but most often it was the older who yielded *voluntarily* to the younger.
- The great majority of the children recovered very quickly after a quarrel and showed no evidence of resentment.

John and Elizabeth Newson found in their 1976 study, *Seven Years Old in the Home Environment*, that two-thirds of their sample of Nottingham seven-year-olds fought sometimes or often with their siblings, and half of these (girls as well as boys) actually came to blows fairly regularly.

Tantrums

Bad tempered reactions to frustration leading to an awesome display of tantrums are common among toddlers, as we have seen. It is not necessarily a sign that a child is especially aggressive. Toddlers have strong wills but have yet to learn self-control. When someone or something stops them from getting their own way, their frustration can build up to explosion point.

Often a child will not be able to explain the particular frustrations which lead up to his/her temper explosion. A parent has to try to 'read' the child to understand the feelings that lie behind the outburst. Parents may not be able to stop their child's tantrums altogether, but they can usually reduce the number and intensity of them. If the child's feelings and needs are taken into account, he or she will not need to explode so often. This does not mean children have to get their own way all the time (see page 97 for some specific tactics).

The antecedents of aggression

The antecedents (stage-setting) for anger and aggression are many and varied, the most basic being the temperamental make up or personality of the child.

Differences in personaltiy, gender and age

Some children are consistently more aggressive than others. Indeed, aggression is one of the most predictable (stable) psychological traits or attributes over the life-span; children who are particularly aggressive at the age of three are also likely to be the children who fight and quarrel most frequently at fourteen and even in early adulthood. There is no reason to be fatalistic. You *can* do something to moderate the anger. But if a child is still *excessively* aggressive and anti-social at six or seven one's mental alarm bells should be sounding; it is time to seek professional help.

I mentioned earlier the finding that (from as early as the second year of life) boys are, on average, more aggressive than girls; and there are also differences in the way in which the sexes express their hostility. With girls the aggression is more likely to consist of a verbal attack. Boys, by and large, express their aggression in physical assault. Some of the differences in aggressiveness between boys and girls may be due to the fact that parents tend to disapprove more of aggression in girls. In our culture females are supposed, by many, to fulfil the role of submissive, gentle and nurturant creatures. Boys are expected to be assertive go-getters, so parents tend to approve of aggression in their male offspring as 'manly'. Much of the time parents are quite unconscious of their 'reinforcing' behaviour.

A psychologist, Florence Goodenough, analysed records of angry outbursts by forty-five American children of from one to seven years of age. Their mothers kept daily diaries of any angry incidents. A total of 1878 angry episodes were recorded over four months. She was able to list the following forms of expression of anger: kicking, stamping, jumping up and down, throwing oneself on the floor, holding one's breath, pulling, struggling, pouting, frowning, throwing objects, grabbing, biting, striking, crying and screaming. Each child had his or her own particular repertoire with a preference for some actions over others, but with time they changed their repertoire. The researcher found that there was a rapid decrease in outbursts as the child got older after the peak age of eighteen months. Boys consistently showed more anger outbursts than girls. As the children increased in age from two to five years, there was a steady diminution in random directionless expressions of anger, and an increase in retaliatory behaviour aimed at someone or something. Fewer than one-third of the outbursts lasted for as long as five minutes.

Lack of social adjustment

The immediate causes of anger could be divided into the following categories, which accounted for the vast majority of incidents reported:

30% Problems of social relationship (e.g. being denied attention, incomprehension of child's desires, etc.)
20% Conflicts over routine physical habits (e.g. going to bed or the toilet, etc.)
20% Conflicts with authority (response to punishment, prohibitions, etc.)

Interference with the satisfaction of needs is one of the many sources of frustration leading to aggression. Problems of social adjustment constituted the most frequent single source of anger outbursts among children.

Much aggression and quarrelsomeness is due to the self-centredness of immaturity. The child is unable to look beyond himself/herself and see things as the other person does. Sharing is rejected. 'That toy is *mine*' – indeed, *your* toy is 'mine' – and the child refuses to take turns (*I* want the swing).

One of the most frequent causes of fighting is the dispute over the possession of desired objects. Self-control obviously enters the picture as the child gets older. Hostility in older children is frequently inhibited from open expression as inner controls are developed. More effective and more socially acceptable ways of solving conflicts are developed and rules governing the rights of persons and property gradually enter a child's awareness. However, at every age there are wide differences among individuals in the circumstances leading to fighting and in the amount of aggressive behaviour displayed.

Sibling jealousy and rivalry

Young children commonly react to the birth of a brother or sister by becoming naughty and demanding, as well as clinging and tearful. Many show open jealousy and tease or irritate the baby. Not all their reactions by any means are negative; you can capitalize (in your efforts to foster understanding and friendship) on any steps they make in the direction of greater independence and on any interest (or overtures of affection) shown towards the infant sibling.

Of course, you must make sure you protect the baby from a toddler who pinches or slaps or tries to tip her out of the pram when your back is turned. But punishing the child, telling him how naughty he is and how disappointed you are that such a big boy is behaving so stupidly, will not solve the problem. It is more likely to increase his anger and feelings of rejection, just when what he needs is reassurance that you will still love him just as much.

Judy Dunn, a Cambridge psychologist, recommends the preparation of your child for the new arrival. As some children are both caring *and* hostile to the baby, you can promote the caring side by attending to it and demonstrating your pleasure at his/her actions. Dr. Dunn believes it is important to provide positive suggestions to your older child about how to handle the new baby. 'Touch or kiss gently' is much better than 'Don't hurt him'. But don't be too easygoing about allowing your child too much freedom with the baby.

When you involve the child with the baby – a desirable strategy – be around to supervise and model (demonstrate) appropriate behaviour. Encourage her to 'help' you with the baby and give her plenty of praise while she is doing it. Once the baby is settled, make sure the child has some time all to herself when she gets a cuddle and your undivided attention. The same applies to older children. A certain amount of rivalry and competition is natural, but all children need to feel that they have their own special talents and that they are not always being measured against brothers or sisters and found wanting. They need to know that a part of your day will be theirs.

It can be an uphill struggle. Interviews with young children indicate that they use far more emotional words to describe their brothers and sisters than to describe friends or even parents. More often than not the words they choose to apply are negative. One-third of five- and six-year-olds in one study said they would prefer to be without their sibling altogether – hardly a vote of confidence in sibship.

A large variety of unpleasant events (what psychologists call 'aversive stimuli') can set the stage for the development of conflict and a chain reaction of quarrelsome behaviours – for example, bullying and teasing of a painful, threatening or humiliating nature; depriving the weaker child of his or her property, rights and opportunities. Obviously it would make sense to remove or reduce (as far as possible) the provocations (antecedents) that lead to bickering, fighting or other forms of dispute.

Who starts the quarrels?

Judy Dunn found that two-year-old second-born children were just as likely as their elders to initiate a quarrel, to tease, and to hit. Mothers were twice as likely to scold the older children and tell them to stop; with younger children, however, they tended not to scold but to distract them and try to interest them in something other than the source of conflict.

Who is responsible for (in the sense of starting) the various quarrels in any family is usually six of one and half a dozen of the other. If you apply the same consequences to both children – say, time-out – not only are you relieved of being judge and jury but you encourage them to avoid fights by co-operating or settling differences peacefully. Co-operation and harmony should therefore be made worthwhile from your children's point of view. In most families the parents tend to pay attention to the children when they quarrel, but to pay much less attention when they are playing peacefully together. This is the time when most parents retire to a comfortable chair or get on with their other jobs. Sadly, there is no respite for parents; *this* is the time that offers a brief opportunity to make an encouraging or acknowledging remark.

Parental hostility

The problems of adolescent aggression, destructiveness and vandalism have been the subject of extensive psychological research. For example, psychologists consistently find that parents of adolescents who are not aggressive rarely reinforce their youngsters for resorting to physical aggression in response to provocation. Aggressive behaviour is penalized. Parents of aggressive teenagers, on the other hand, tolerate no aggressive displays whatsoever in the *home*, but condone, indeed, actively encourage and reinforce, provocation and aggressive actions towards others in the *community*.

A combination of lax discipline and hostile attitudes on the part of both parents encourages very aggressive and poorly controlled behaviour in their offspring. The pattern of child-rearing that produces the most hostile children is one where the parents use punitive methods persistently against a background of rejecting, hostile parental attitudes. These methods are often referred to as power-assertive; the adult asserts dominant and authoritarian control through physical punishment, harsh verbal abuse, angry threats and deprivation of privileges.

Later on I shall move to a closer look at adolescents; adolescence, although a *continuation* of childhood (and we must never forget that), does generate special disciplinary issues of its own, so it deserves a chapter to itself (chapter 10).

Parental intervention in quarrels

We have examined some of the antecedents to aggressive actions. What of the consequences of fighting? For example, there is some disagreement about how wise it is for parents to intervene in their children's quarrels, given that parental attention might unwittingly reinforce quarrelling.

Quarrelling might well increase in frequency if each child observes the other being reprimanded or getting the parent – even temporarily – to take his or her side. The counter-argument is that parental intervention is necessary to teach values of fair play, sharing and compromise. Many parents feel, too, that if they *don't* intervene, hurt and/or an injustice will be done to the younger and/or weaker child. Nor do they wish to condone the use of fighting or bullying by default, which means inaction.

Judy Dunn has reviewed several studies of parental intervention and non-intervention. On the one hand, studies in which parents were trained to stay right out of brotherly and sisterly quarrels seem to indicate that the frequency of such arguments can be reduced – particularly if ignoring quarrels is combined with rewarding the children for desisting from conflict. On the other hand, other studies indicate that, if parents wish to encourage in children an ability to care about what happens to other people, they need to point out clearly and forcefully to their offspring, when young, the consequences of being unkind and aggressive. Quarrels between brothers and sisters provide the ideal training-ground to carry out this kind of teaching.

Judy Dunn and a co-worker observed directly the interactions of brothers and sisters in their own homes, in forty-three pairs of siblings. In each pair the younger child was eighteen months old. They revisited six months later to make further observations. The mothers' behaviour was also recorded. What did they find out?

- There was a good deal of quarrelling – an average of about eight fights, or potential fights, per hour.
- It did seem that the mother's intrusion in quarrels led to more conflict over the longer term.
- In families where the mother tended to intervene often in the first observation period, the children did have longer quarrels and more frequent physical fights in the second observation period (six months later) than in families where she intervened less.

- There was also evidence that, when a mother adopted a style of discussing rules and feelings with the children when they quarrelled, they were apt to develop in their offspring more mature ways of handling conflict. These included conciliatory actions such as showing concern for, comforting, helping or apologizing to the other. Their children were more likely to refer to rules. ('We have to take turns. Mummy said so.')

How do you plan your actions on the basis of what seems like a contradiction in this and other research? On the one hand (see page 31) reasoning with children, and helping them recognize others' feelings, facilitates the development of conscience and resistance to temptation. On the other hand (see page 46) reasoning with children involves giving them a great deal of attention which might reinforce and maintain, if not increase, the quarrelsomeness. Perhaps the lesson for parents is to ignore the quarrel at the time (if no harm is being caused) but get both children together later on and discuss how they might have settled their differences. Since there is evidence that at least some quarrels are attempts to attract attention or are bids for the parents' favour, make it clear from the outset that while you are not interested in hearing the details of arguments, or the telling of tales, you will not tolerate any hitting. Ignoring disputes for the moment will be crucial if you have an inkling that your children squabble more when you are around.

Chapter Nine

Controlling anger and aggression

Tactics for dealing with aggressive children

Up to now I have suggested some general strategies for pre-empting or cooling down quarrels and temper outbursts. But what about specific, all-purpose tactics? I have tried to emphasize the *positive* in this book, and in that spirit I should like to repeat that the longer term counter to fighting, jealousy and acquisitiveness is to *train* the child, patiently and repetitively, to share, to wait patiently, to see that pulling hair hurts, to co-operate – in other words to be socially sensitive. Judy Dunn has invaluable advice for parents on this theme in her book *The Beginnings of Social Understanding*: The point is that co-operative behaviour is incompatible with aggression and for this reason increasing co-operative activities by reinforcing them is one very effective way of diminishing aggression.

An investigation of nursery school children demonstrated that their teachers were able to halve the frequency of fights and quarrels merely by attending to the children when they were playing peacefully, and offering comments such as 'That's nice', 'You *are* playing well together'.

If your child seems unable to play without quarrelling you could try a 'token economy', as it is called. If he/she can play with brothers and sisters (or friends) for, say, half an hour without squabbling, you call him/her over quietly and award an agreed number of tokens (see page 57–9).

Increasing awareness of others

Teach your child to see the other person's point of view (not necessarily at the expense of his or her own). Role-taking – the mental placing of oneself in the other person's position – is central to all forms of human communication. There is evidence that very early in life children engage in rudimentary forms of role-taking particularly during play: playing mother or nurse or teacher. Nevertheless, when children are confronted with points of view that are different from their own, they often assume similarity where there is none. This can lead to misunderstanding, mutual frustration, anger, quarrelling and perhaps aggression. In order to develop social awareness – which means a consciousness of other people's roles, rights, needs and sensitivities – the following steps may be taken:

- Praise the child for initiating social behaviour.
- Model (i.e. demonstrate) social behaviour to a child.
- Physically demonstrate various ways of interacting socially with others, indicate how she might make positive comments about another child, and show her how to play constructively.
- Ask him to demonstrate something to another child (e.g. how to work the fizzy-drinks machine); direct her to help, or seek help, of another.
- Coach the child in social behaviour: encourage her in social activity and describe or explain ways of interacting socially (e.g. when she is with children parents have invited home).
- Encourage the child to adopt a sociable perspective (e.g. 'Let's talk about how you can have fun with other kids when you play games'; 'One way of making a game fun for everyone is to take turns ... when you take turns in a game other kids will have fun too and will want to play with you again').

Stress management: the turtle technique

Training children in self-control and relaxation techniques gives them control over actual or potentially stressful situations that lead to aggression or (incidentally) fearful panic. It is those situations which are beyond our control which people find most alarming. Suggesting something which the child can *say* to himself/herself in a crisis ('self-talk') can be surprisingly helpful: 'I am in control; I can manage. I am not going to be provoked.' Suggesting something which he or she can *do* – some *action* – adds to the child's sense of mastery.

The turtle technique is a simple self-control technique children can be taught to use when they feel themselves becoming tense or angry. It is an imaginative combination of *'self-talk'* (or 'self-instruction') and *action* (in the form of relaxation and problem-solving methods).

The Schneider and Robin turtle technique begins with a story to tell young children about a boy called Little Turtle. Little Turtle disliked school. In spite of his vows to stay out of trouble he always managed to find it. For example, he would get angry and rip up all his papers in class. One day when he was feeling especially bad, he met a talking tortoise. The old tortoise addressed him: 'Hey, there, I'll tell you a secret. don't you realize you are carrying the answer to your problem around with you?' Little Turtle didn't know what he was talking about. 'Your shell – your shell!' the tortoise shouted in his loud bellowing tones. 'That's why you have a shell. You can hide in your shell whenever you get that feeling inside you that tells you you are angry. When you are in your shell, you can have a moment to rest and figure out what to do about it. So next time you get angry, just go into your shell.'

The story continues with an account of how the next day when he started to get upset Little Turtle remembered what the tortoise had told him so he closed his eyes, pulled in his arms close to his body, put his head down so his chin rested against his chest, and rested for a while, until he knew what to do. The story ends with the teacher coming over and praising him for this reaction and Little Turtle receiving a very good report card that term.

The story is thus used to teach a child to respond like the wise old tortoise when the cue word 'turtle' is given. After the child has mastered the turtle response through modelling and rehearsing, a relaxation process of tensing and relaxing body muscles is taught.

The story is resumed where Little Turtle returns to the tortoise, telling him that he still has some angry feelings, even though he has used the turtle response. The children are given practice in tensing and relaxing major muscle groups of their body, starting with the stomach muscles. Tensing and relaxation are then incorporated into the turtle response by tensing the body when assuming the turtle position, as a count is made from one to ten, followed by relaxation of the muscles, which is maintained for a few moments. The children are encouraged to use frustrating experiences as a cue to employ the turtle reaction.

Learning the turtle reaction is combined with teaching the child problem-solving skills, during which recent problem situations are discussed. Cues are provided for the children, such as the teacher asking 'What are your choices?' The children are instructed to incorporate problem-solving efforts during use of the turtle technique; that is, to use this time to imagine alternative reactions to their frustrating situation and the consequences of each. In this way, the child learns to expand his/her range of *alternative coping* strategies.

You can use the word 'turtle' to prompt a child to go into the turtle reactions to avoid impulsive aggression. Eventually you reinforce the child for using the turtle response spontaneously in conflict situations. Some children report doing 'turtle in my head' without prompting and without going through the physical turtle response for self-control. The results reported by Schneider and Robin indicate that aggression and tantrums decreased by 46 per cent and 54 per cent in two elementary school classrooms for the emotionally disturbed after eight weeks of training using the turtle technique.

Identifying stressful situations

Your child or teenager may find the following method helpful. He/she sits down with you and compiles a list of the situations and circumstances which make them angry (being criticized at school, being called names, and so on). Each situation is then rated on a five point scale according to whether it just bothers them a little or makes them really angry. This technique will help your youngster (and, indeed, yourself) to become more sensitive to 'explosive' situations where he or she will most need to exercise self-control. You can use the rating scale to monitor changes over time in your youngster's ability to cope with provocations.

Distraction

You can often distract your child before his rage builds up to bursting point. If you have to stop him doing one thing, provide something else to interest and occupy him. Once he is in the grip of a real temper tantrum, it is useless to try punishing him, since he is beyond all reason, unable to understand what he is doing or what you are saying. There can come a point when a child is genuinely beside himself (you have to use your knowledge of your child) and you need to encompass him firmly in your arms until he calms down.

Ignoring

If you begin to feel your child is using tantrums to manipulate you, if an element of 'acting up' has shown itself, ignore her (see page 46) and leave the room. Actors need audiences and she will soon get bored with performing all alone. A toddler who learns that a fit of anger or temper brings her mother's anxious ministrations, or the limelight of being the centre of attention for a roomful of people, will work herself up into more tempers. If she learns that they bring her nothing but exhaustion, she will try to avoid them.

Discouraging aggressive behaviour

At all costs aggressive behaviour must not be allowed to be rewarding. It is a risky policy merely to ignore really aggressive behaviour, simply to let children or teenagers fight it out to the finish. Left to themselves, without adult interference, groups of children tend to become more rather than less aggressive as time goes by. Aggression has its own rewards, which leads to its perpetuation. Gerald Patterson and his psychologist colleagues in Oregon, USA, observing children in nursery schools, found that 80 per cent of aggressive behaviour had some positive reward or payoff for the aggressor; for example, the victim gave up a toy, or cried, or ran away.

There is a view, which is both popular and respectable, that childhood games of murder and mayhem and also the watching of portrayed violence, can exert a positive effect through 'catharsis'. Emotions (according to this theory) are purged because of the release of tension involved in identifying with the participants in a representation of violent events. Anger is 'drained off', so to speak, by 'living through' (in imagination) or 'acting out' these situations. In a variation of this theme, some parents argue that it is 'therapeutic' for their child to express aggression towards them because they are bound to frustrate the child at times. This channelled expression of anger is supposed to be 'healthier' than its inhibition. There are at least two reasons to question the assumptions underlying such notions.

First, there is little place in a civilized, co-operative society for the direct and unrestrained expression of aggression, whether it is physical or verbal attack. Some 'disguised' forms of verbal aggression, such as gossip or 'calling a spade a spade', are tolerated to a greater degree than physical attack or direct verbal abuse, but even gossip and frankness that conceal hostility are likely to produce complications in human relationships.

Second, the expression of aggression and its consequent momentary release of tension strengthens rather than weakens the tendency to behave aggressively (see page 80). There is no evidence to indicate that behaving aggressively reduces tendencies to be aggressive. If anything, studies suggest the opposite: children and young adults with crude fantasies of aggression have been found to be more openly aggressive in their behaviour than those whose aggressive fantasies are muted or contain elements indicating that they are as concerned with the dangerous consequences of their aggression as they are with the aggression itself. In other words, aggressive fantasy *may suggest* or stimulate aggressive behaviour, rather than drain off the motive to behave aggressively.

There are undoubtedly risks in encouraging children to redirect their hostility rather than getting to the root of the problem (if aggression is frequent and/or intense) or training the child in ways of coping with life that don't involve aggression.

Self-help for parents

Parents have feelings and they have rights too (or they should have!). They get tired, frustrated, irritable and downright incensed at times. So your child may not be the only one who needs to boost his or her self-control by counting up to ten, playing turtle or learning to relax. You may find your temper on a short fuse when confronting your child or teenager for the umpteenth time. There are several methods you may find helpful when you feel you are losing control or when you are at a loss to understand your child's persistent aggression.

Self-instruction (self-talk)

There are times when parents get so angry with their children that they are in danger of losing their self-control. A psychologist, R. H. Novaco, provides us with positive self-statements (which I have abbreviated) for dealing with anger:

- *Preparing for provocation*
  This is going to upset me, but I know how to deal with it.
  What is it that I have to do?
  I can manage the situation, I know how to regulate my anger.

If I find myself getting upset, I'll know what to do.
Try not to take this too seriously.
Time for a few deep breaths of relaxation.
Easy does it. Remember to keep your sense of humour.

- *Reacting during the confrontations*
Stay calm. Just continue to relax.
As long as I keep my cool, I'm in control.
Think of what you want to get out of this.
There is no point in getting mad.
Don't make more out of this than you have to.
I'm not going to let him get to me.
Look for the positives. Don't assume the worst or jump to conclusions.
It's really a shame that she has to act like this.
If I start to get mad, I'll just be banging my head against the wall. So I might as well just relax.
I'm on top of this situation and it's under control.

- *Coping with arousal*
My muscles are starting to feel tight. Time to relax and slow things down.
Getting upset won't help.
It's just not worth it to get so angry.
I have a right to be annoyed, but let's keep the lid on.
Time to take a deep breath.
Let's take the issue point by point.
My anger is a signal of what I need to do. Time to instruct myself.
Try to reason it out. Treat each other with respect.
Let's try a co-operative approach. Maybe we are both right.
Negatives lead to more negatives. Work constructively.
He'd probably like me to get really angry. Well I'm going to disappoint him.

- *Reflecting on the experience*

When conflict is unresolved:

Forget about the aggravation. Thinking about it only makes you upset.

Self-help for parents

These are difficult situations, and they take time to straighten out.
I'll get better at this as I get more practice.
Remember relaxation. It's a lot better than anger.
Can you laugh about it? It's probably not so serious.
Don't take it personally.
Take a deep breath and think positive thoughts.

When conflict is resolved or coping is successful:

I handled that one pretty well. It worked!
That wasn't as hard as I thought.
It could have been a lot worse.
I actually got through that without getting angry.
I guess I've been getting upset for too long when it wasn't even necessary.
I'm doing better at this all the time.

Relaxation

The following exercises are suggested by Reg Beech, a clinical psychologist, for coping with stress and tension. The exercises all involve the following general steps:

- Lightly tense a given group of muscles (as listed below) and hold this tension for a slow count of five while holding your breath.
- During the above step, focus your attention on the sensations in the part of your body that has been brought under tension.
- At the end of five seconds, breathe out, relax the tense muscles *as much as possible*, focusing your mind on the new relaxed sensations in that part of your body.
- While letting go (as above), think of the words 'calm yourself' and 'relax'.
- Allow your muscles to relax completely and, in your mind,

compare the feelings of tension just experienced with the relaxation you now feel.

The particular exercises are as follows:

Arms: Clench the fists and tighten the muscles of both arms, holding your arms still and straight out in front of you.

Legs: Raise both legs (or one, if preferred) about 12–18 inches from their resting position, point the toes and stiffen the legs so that thigh and calf muscles are brought under tension. Repeat with the other leg if necessary.

General torso: Pull the shoulders back, bringing shoulder blades together, push the chest forward and out and, at the same time, use appropriate muscles to *pull in* the stomach, making a hollow in that part of your body.

Neck: Press the head firmly against the support of the chair back or mattress.

Face: There are three separate exercises here:
- Raise the eyebrows, forcing them up as far as you can as if trying to make them meet your hair line.
- Screw up your eyes tightly and, at the same time, wrinkle your nose and compress lips hard.
- Clench the jaws, as if chewing hard, while pushing your tongue hard against the roof of your mouth.

Remember, each of the above exercises is immediately preceded by taking a deep breath, creating tension, and holding it for five seconds, then exhaling while letting go the tension and saying the word 'relax' to yourself. In each case try to focus your mind on the part of your body that has in turn been made tense and relaxed.

Don't try to hurry the programme of exercises, which should take about twenty minutes or so. After each separate exercise allow a minute or so for fuller relaxation to take place and for you to concentrate on the pleasant sensations that relaxation brings. Most people need about three weeks of daily training to achieve a useful level of skill, but don't stop at that point.

Problem-solving

An analysis of aggressive episodes could help you to work out a practical campaign to deal with a persistent problem over discipline. The following steps provide a guide to action.

Step 1 Ask yourself: what *precisely* is it that my child is doing wrong? If your answer is vague (e.g. 'He is always disobedient'), it is impossible to plan your strategy and tactics to bring about change. If, however, your answer is specific (e.g. 'She has a temper tantrum when I insist that she obeys me, for example when I tell her to eat up her breakfast') then an effective procedure can be worked out. Before you can change your child's behaviour you have to look at that behaviour very closely. Let's take temper tantrums as an example, and work through the remaining steps.

Step 2 Observe the tantrums carefully. You must describe to yourself *precisely* what behaviour it is that you are going to observe.

Q What is it your child *does* and *says* that makes you refer to his/her actions/words as a temper tantrum?
A She stamps her foot, clenches her fists, kicks the chairs. She also screams and swears.

Stamping, fist-clenching, kicking, screaming and swearing are our target behaviours (the ones to be concentrated on).

Step 3 Observe how frequently your child loses his/her temper. *Count* the number of tantrums (defined by those actions you described) that he/she has per day. Do this for a few days (see figure 4).

Step 4 Keep a brief diary record of each episode, with particular emphasis on the sequence of behaviour (figure 5 illustrates this):

A What led up to the
B tantrum?
C What happened immediately afterwards?

Mandy's chart   Date: Week:

Time	Mon.	Tues.	Wed.	Thurs.	Fri.	Sat.	Sun.
7–8	T, D	C	T, D / T	D / T	D, T	C	C
8–9	C		T	T	T, D		
9–10						T	
10–11							
11–12							
12–1						D, T	D
1–2							
2–3							
3–4							
4–5	D / T	D, T	D	D, T	D		
5–6	T, T	T, T	D, T	T	T	D, T	D
6–7		D	T (long one 25 mins)	T	C		C
7–8							C

Key   T = temper tantrum = Mandy screams, lies on the floor, kicking, banging her head, banging her fists.

D = disobedience/defiance = M ignores request (i.e. after one repetition). M says 'no'/ shakes head – refuses to obey.

C = co-operation behaviour = M helps mother (or others) as defined in contract.

Figure 4 *Daily counting chart to show how often a child does something within a given period of time*
Source: M. Herbert, *Behavioural Treatment of Children with Problems* (London: Academic Press, 1987)

Step 5 Analyse your information, first the antecedents.

Q When you look at your diary after a few days, and your tally of tantrums, are they part of a *more general pattern*? (Are the antecedents, rather similar?)'

A Yes, they seem to form a pattern of defiance. They follow two lines: either my child commands me to do something, and if I don't, she insists, and eventually has a tantrum;

Self-help for parents

Time	Antecedent: what happens beforehand?	Client behaviour	Consequences: what happens next?
9.p.m	Mother asks Avril to put her toys away.	Avril takes no notice	Mother tidies them up.
9.30 p.m	Father tells Avril to go to bed.	Avril says, 'I don't want to, just give me a little while more.'	There is a debate: 1. Father tells her it is late (she ignores). 2. Mother pleads. Avril ignores. There is a heated exchange. 1. Mother scolds. 2. Father shouts. Avril is given ten more minutes.

Figure 5 *Diary record of behaviour sequences*
Source: M. Herbert, *Working with Children and their Families* (London: Routledge/British Psychological Society, 1988)

or I ask her to do something and she ignores me or says, 'I won't!'. If I insist, she has a tantrum.

Step 6   Find out how specific the tantrums are.

Q When you look at your tally do the tantrums seem more *frequent*?
- at certain times?
- in certain places?
- in particular situations?

A The answer in this case is *yes* to all those questions. They are most frequent in the morning and at night; in the bedroom, at the dinner table; with me; when I try to dress her, get her to eat up her meal, or put away her toys.

Step 7   Analyse the consequences. For example, have you slipped into the habit of simply repeating your commands parrot-like – over and over again – without really expecting any result? Do you always give way, perhaps because it's the easiest thing to do? (Anything for a quiet life!)

Q Looking at your diary again, can you see any kind of pattern in the consequences or outcomes to these trying confrontations?

A Yes, my child usually gets her own way – not always, but nearly always. She also gets me going. I sometimes end up in tears. She *always* gets me into an argument and I have to devote a lot of time to the dispute.

Step 8 Identify the reinforcers. In this case, *you* (and others) have unwittingly reinforced (strengthened) the very behaviours (tantrums) that you wished to weaken and reduce in frequency. The reinforcers are as follows:

- She gets her own way.
- She riles you and enjoys getting a rise out of you.
- She has monopolized your attention; even if it is scolding it is rewarding (after all the behaviour is as *persistent* as ever).

Step 9 Be quite clear in your mind how your child must change in order for the situation to improve. Also be specific. For example: I expect her to obey me when I make a reasonable request or command, so that, if (say) I ask her to remain at the table until she's finished her meal, she does so without endless arguments or fits of temper.

Step 10 Retrain your child. There are two general principles involved in putting right the unsatisfactory situation we have gradually disentangled and thus clarified. In retraining your child you will have to:

- *weaken* the undesirable actions;
- *strengthen* a desirable action that is incompatible (i.e. competes) with the undesirable one.

Think of a desired alternative action – one that cannot be performed at the same time as the 'problem' behaviour (see page 55). She cannot help you pack your box at the supermarket and have a tantrum at the same time. Remember to reinforce (words of praise, cuddles, a star for a star chart) the actions – and you may have to prompt her, at first – that compete with having tantrums, i.e. acts of compliance and co-operation. If she goes through the checkout without a tantrum praise her behaviour ('You're a big girl behaving so well'). Give her a symbolic reward (a star on her chart) when she gets home and a tangible one (a biscuit) *as* you leave the shop. Repeat your *reasons* for this acknowledgement. Gradually you should be able to phase out the tangible reinforcers when tantrums are no longer a major part of her repertoire. Make sure that *no* instance of her tantrums receives any reinforcement! In other words, you weaken the tantrums by not reinforcing (rewarding) them. You might ignore the tantrum, turn your back on it, or you might use 'time-out' (see figure 3 on page 72).

If you do decide to use time-out, explain *once* why you are going to use it; give *one* warning only of the imminence of time-out, each time she begins a tantrum. *Do not scold or dispute on the way to, or during time-out*. Be gentle, but matter of fact and very firm. Do persist! Some behaviours change only slowly. If you take the line of least resistance or fail to be consistent, you will actually make things worse.

Chapter Ten

Discipline for teenagers

Many of the tips provided so far for the management of children have been relevant for adolescents. This is particularly the case with general principles such as making desirable behaviour worthwhile, setting limits and having clearly defined but fair rules of conduct.

But adolescence presents quite different problems regarding discipline. For one thing, you are dealing (in the later teens) with a young adult. Bearing that in mind, the style of communication you adopt with your youngster could save you a lot of aggravation and heartache. Nevertheless, teenagers, because of their immaturity and inexperience, still need the following:

- supervision (not surveillance);
- rules (i.e. reasonable but firm limits);
- guidance (your experience/advice can be helpful in preventing serious mistakes/dangers);
- someone to talk to and confide in;
- love, encouragement and reassurance.

With teenagers you have to bear in mind that:

- they are capable of much more sophisticated thinking than previously (which means the likelihood of involved debates and arguments);
- they are driven by a mixture of physical and psychological longings and apprehensions which can result in moodiness, aloofness, irritability, hostility, insecurity and (at times) sheer delightfulness;
- they need you more than you think and they will admit;

- they are trying out different 'personalities' as they prepare for adulthood;
- they are caught, often, in a conflict between holding on to the security of their childhood dependence and striking out for independence.

Responsibility and freedom

If you give your teenage son or daughter a sense of responsibility, they are likely to become responsible adults. Of course, it takes time: experience is a matter of learning by one's mistakes; and naturally you wish to protect your child from serious mistakes and dangers. But if you always treat them as too young or too feckless to have your trust or good opinion, they are likely to stay immature and irresponsible.

Guideline 22: Give your youngster the chance to be responsible by giving him/her responsibility.

The best way of learning certain 'lessons' is to be asked to teach them to someone else. This is why the responsibility of (say) looking after a small brother or sister is so valuable in enhancing the social awareness and maturity of the older boy or girl who is doing the substitute parenting.

A teenager who feels she has a share in making family policies is far more likely to accept the need to give and take, balancing her wants and needs with those of her parents. She is far more likely to obey the rules if you discuss them with her, so that she knows why you make them.

Guideline 23: Include your teenager in family discussions.

Adolescents are very sensitive about pretence, hypocrisy or deceit on the part of their parents. If you give them an explanation which later turns out to be untrue, their trust in you is shaken, their sense of security undermined, and they will not easily forgive you. Sometimes parents fail to give the true reason why something upsets them because they think the youngster is not old enough to know about such things. If she starts talking about sexual matters they may jump in hastily, saying, 'Don't talk about that' without explaining why they are disturbed by what she has said. Dodging the issue like this only creates feelings of confusion, guilt or resentment.

Traditionally parents have tried to keep a lot of information about life and about their own affairs from their children. But this sort of secrecy can often produce more anxiety than if parents explain the facts clearly and simply. For instance, if father has lost his job, whispered conversations about money worries, which break off as soon as children come near, may give them the idea that a terrible disaster is about to strike, or even that they are too insignificant to be taken into their parents' confidence. Teenagers (and children) should always be told about future events involving them – moving house, or father going into hospital for an operation – so that they have time to adjust to the idea. If you give them time and sufficient explanation and preparation, children can deal surprisingly well with crises in their lives. They suffer far more psychological shock if an event hits them out of the blue.

As children get older, it helps to hold short family meetings to discuss matters like holidays, which concern the whole family, and talk over anything which is important to the child – her pocket money or when to return home from a party.

Guideline 24: Tell your teenager how you feel.

Listening carefully to what your son or daughter has to say (his or her opinions, feelings and difficulties) is only one part of good communication. *You* should also have the right and freedom to express your own feelings in a frank manner, without feeling guilty. Not only you but also your teenager will benefit from such honesty. You are demonstrating to them how to recognize, name and communicate their feelings without going overboard.

Psychologists refer to these statements about one's own feelings as 'I' messages. If your daughter comes home late yet again, you might say 'When you come home late at night I am worried sick. And then – after I know you are safe – my anxiety turns into resentment. I feel angry and let down by you.' This is preferable to shouting 'You're nothing but an untrustworthy young madam! You're becoming nothing but a delinquent!'

'You are' messages often have the effect of attaching negative descriptions or labels to the young person's character: 'You are thoroughly bad'; 'You're the most conceited, selfish person I've ever known'. The trouble is that the awful things parents say about their children, often repeated, not usually 'meant' except in the heat of the moment, tend to stick. They are taken seriously by many children, who come to believe them and, indeed, act on them. Call a child stupid often enough, and she will act as if she were stupid, which almost amounts to becoming stupid. Call a teenager bad often enough, treat him as someone who is bad and he is likely to fulfil your 'prophecy'. One's behaviour is strongly determined by what one *believes* of oneself, as well as what one *is*. This psychological finding provides us with our next cautionary guideline:

Guideline 25: Refrain from sticking negative 'labels' to your teenager's personality.

Throughout this book I have suggested that it is important, in training children, to convey a reasonably coherent idea of the aims and objects that lie behind the training and supervision.

Children whose parents set firm limits for them grow up with more self-esteem and confidence than those who are allowed to get away with behaving in any way they like. It is important to give the youngster a reasonable amount of freedom of choice within those limits. These principles shouldn't be forgotten or cease to be put into effect simply because your child is becoming a young adult.

Guideline 26: Continue to make firm moral and social demands.

Teenagers who get their own way all the time interpret such *laissez-faire* permissiveness as indifference. So, if you have to cope with recrimination, invidious comparisons and abuse from your son or daughter, take the long view and remain solid and safe; it may be painful for you, but it will pay off in the longer term.

Contracts and negotiations

One of the factors contributing to the disciplinary problems of young people is their inability to cope with conflicts involving authority figures – those interpersonal occasions in which the youth and an authority figure (such as a parent or teacher) have opposing desires. The youth may want to buy a motor bike, but his mother wants him to purchase an old car because she thinks bikes are dangerous and will get him into bad company.

Teenagers often make inappropriate responses to conflicts such as aggression, withdrawing, sulking, tantrums or destructive behaviour. Negotiation could sometimes defuse these situations and produce more acceptable consequences for both parties.

At a time of crisis when teenagers and their parents (or brothers and sisters) are at loggerheads, angry and resentful, contracts provide an opportunity for the family to take stock and to break through vicious circles of retribution and unreason. Although it probably sounds odd that I am suggesting negotiating a written agreement with your teenager, psychologists have been using business-style contracts to resolve family conflicts for some years now. Contracts, it may be thought, are the domain of lawyers or salesmen – far too cold and commercial to apply to human relationships. However, it is precisely because a contract is such a detached, objective way of dealing with emotional issues that it can work. Just sitting down together as a family to draft an agreement can encourage analysis and co-operation. It is an invaluable 'workshop' in which to teach your teenager the art of compromise.

Guideline 27: Teach your teenager the art of compromise.

Take the Grant family, for example. At first their difficulties seemed insurmountable. Nearly all of them expressed unhappiness or discontent, particularly teenager Anne, who was threatening to leave home. Her mother, Avril, felt trapped, tired and depressed, hemmed in by the demands of a fretful strong-willed toddler, ten-year-old John, who was beginning to refuse to go to school, and her 'selfish' husband, James. He, meanwhile, was feeling thoroughly middle-aged, and worried about his health and the possibility of redundancy. In his opinion, he received little attention from his wife: 'She's completely wrapped up in the children. All I get is criticism.' Only the grandmother seemed above it all, but in private she confided that the atmosphere of bickering recrimination made her feel sad and insecure.

In the Grants' case, 'contract sessions' were organized in their own home and were chaired by me. Alternatively, a chair could be elected from within the family; if the person acting as chair varied, a teenager could be given a valuable chance to assume and exercise responsibility.

Patterns of family behaviour evolve gradually until they become unconscious habits. Statements that pass for communication, as the Grants came to realize, are often punitive messages. 'You're always undermining me,' Avril accused

James when he tried to respond to an earlier complaint she had made ('You always opt out at the first hint of difficulty'), and she reprimanded the children. Affectionate words reinforcing 'good' behaviour were notable by their absence.

Conflict – as the Grants slowly realized – is not a matter of words alone; actions too can serve as a trigger for a negative response. Often the things that people don't say – the non-verbal 'cues' – are as destructive as verbal ones. Lack of eye contact from his mother when he was talking about his day gave John Grant the firm message that she had no interest.

The contracts that the Grants finally drew up took five sessions of three quarters of an hour each, but after the initial, inevitable slanging match the sessions were amicable. Having accepted the ground rules, all the Grants appreciated and relished a structure that allowed a degree of communication they had been missing for years. Old grievances and resentments tumbled out, but in the light of day turned out to have less power than when they'd been hidden away. James and Avril Grant, for instance, discovered that their fears of what Anne got up to at night were often unfounded or even ludicrous. Anne herself found that when she voiced her grievances quietly and calmly, rather than screaming them, her family paid attention to her for the first time.

Eventually the family decided that they needed two contracts, one between James and Avril, the other between Anne and her parents. Specific rewards, such as praise, pocket money or sympathy, were built in. (See Anne's contract, which is the one we are interested in as a disciplinary exercise.) These, it must be emphasized, should be seen as privileges rather than automatic rights. They depend on an appropriate display of responsible behaviour, and the circumstances in which they are to be given must be made explicit.

Contract between James and Avril Grant and Anne

Anne will endeavour to:

- Let her parents know about her movements when she goes out at night; she will tell them where she is and with whom, and let them know what time she'll be home.
- Be less moody; she won't sulk when reprimanded or thwarted.
- Be more ready to say sorry; she will apologize when she's been in the wrong.
- Show more concern about her school work; do at least half an hour's homework a night.
- Stop being so rude to her father – walking out when he gives her advice.

Anne would like her parents to:

- Stop criticizing her friends. Admit when they are in the wrong and be ready to apologize.
- Give her more pocket money (a sum agreed) and review the amount every six months in the light of rising expenses and changes in her commitments.

All agree:

- that the terms of the contract will not be changed except by mutual discussion and agreement.
- that disputes will be settled by the witness (grandmother), whom all agree to be objective and fair-minded.
- that successful execution of the contract for a month will be rewarded by a family treat (first month: an outing to a favourite restaurant).
- that failure to carry out individual terms of the contract will result in a fine on each occasion: an amount of X for Anne; and Y for Avril and James Grant, respectively. The money is to go in a penalty box kept by Grandmother; the proceeds will go to a charity.

Success came overnight in neither case; but a slow and steady improvement did take place, hauled back on to the right track at intervals by taking out the original contract and referring yet again to the agreed terms. Little by little the Grants began to do more things together as they came to trust each other, and to find enjoyment in each other's company. John's incipient school problems were nipped in the bud. Anne realized that she didn't really want to leave – she'd just wanted a happier home.

The system of analysing common conflicts that the Grants learnt can be applied to a range of disciplinary and family problems. Certain commonsense ground rules should be mentioned – discussing marital and financial problems with children, for example, is not advisable. Secondly, it is better to focus on a specific cause of concern rather than a sense of general discontent. With more serious problems it would be wise to seek professional counselling.

Should you, having thought it over, wish to try a family contract, there are several points to bear in mind.

- Keep discussion positive. Recriminations are unavoidable, but try to keep their volume down and turn negative complaints into positive suggestions ('You never help with the washing-up' can be turned into a helping rota or rewards).
- Be very specific in spelling out desired actions, avoid being vague (not 'I wish she'd be more helpful' but 'I wish she'd help me with the weekend shopping').
- Pay attention to the details of privileges and conditions for both parties. They should (a) be important, not trivial and (b) make sense to the person involved. For example, you will allow your teenage daughter to stay out after twelve on a Saturday night, if she goes with friends you know and comes home in a taxi, and never alone.
- Encourage positive action if you wish your child or partner to desist from certain activities. Be sure that you spell out specific words and deeds: if a teenager complains about a younger sibling, ask him or her to take the child on an outing.

Contracts and negotiations

- Choose changes you want to bring about that can easily be monitored. If you can't see whether an obligation has been met, you can't readily grant a privilege. You cannot tell if a youngster really has, for instance, stopped smoking; but you will know if your teenager gets in at the negotiated time.
- Make clear to all concerned the penalty for breaking the contract.
- Be careful not to qualify praise (do not, for instance, say, 'Thank you for taking out the rubbish – why don't you do that all the time?').
- Remember that the contract you draw up must embody the principles of mutual caring. If it doesn't, it is a waste of time.
- Keep sessions relatively brief – around forty-five minutes. If the are longer, people start to get tired.
- Keep a diary of progress. I have also found it helpful, during the contract discussion period, if family members write down five specific things they'd like to see changed.

Do remember that it is not only the signed and sealed contract that helps to concentrate people's minds on their commitments. It is the process of actually sitting down as a family – the shared activities of discussing common goals, of settling differences amicably and of treating one another with respect and dignity – that has a healing and constructive part to play.

Teaching your teenager how to negotiate is implicit in the process of formulating a contract. Your best setting for demonstrating the art of negotiation is the one in which you and your son or daughter disagree over some issue. As on page 114 you put your position and make explicit your attitudes and feelings. For example, disputes often arise over an adolescent's room, the parent might say: 'I want you to keep your room clean and tidy. When I see the squalor of your room which is filthy, and has your clothes all over the floor, frankly I get fed up'. The parent should then invite the teenager to give his/her viewpoint, and the teenager may reply: 'I am satisfied with my room as it is. As it's *my* private place, I should be able to do with it as I please.' The parent should listen quietly to this opinion, preferably with an open mind, trying to see things from the youngster's point of view and should restate what she or he understands to be the youngster's argument, so as to be sure of there being no misunderstanding. The parent could then suggest a compromise, such as 'I will undertake not to go into your room, then I won't feel upset and can't nag you. What about your taking responsibility for cleaning the room once a week and looking after your clothes by hanging them up?' Other solutions could be explored. If (hopefully) a solution is reached, the approach you adopted for working through the conflict is discussed. It has three stages:

- State frankly but quietly what you think.
- Listen attentively and quietly to what your teenager thinks.
- Think of different ways of tackling the conflict, of narrowing the gap between points of view. (Parent: 'Now we know more about what each of us feels, can you think of anything else we could do or say so we don't get into this disagreement again?')
- Explore the consequences of each possibility. Will the compromise work? (Parent: 'Can you think of anything that might go wrong if we adopt that course of action?')

Obviously some situations are much more serious and therefore more difficult to resolve than a dispute over an untidy room. The issue may be about an undesirable friendship, being out late at night, buying a motor bike, drinking alcohol, and so on.

Guideline 28: Encourage (by example) your teenager to negotiate.

It is well to prepare your ground when tackling your discussion:

Contracts and negotiations

1 Work out your feelings and attitudes about the situation.

- I feel ... (e.g. 'I feel worried sick')
- When ... (e.g. 'when Liz stays out late')
- Because ... (e.g. 'I don't know if she's safe')

2 Decide whether the particular situation is worth bothering about.

Reasons for: She may get into bad company and be at risk in some way.

Reasons against: There'll be an awful row if I broach the subject.

3 Make an approach.

- Express your own feelings in an unprovocative manner.
- Listen carefully to the reply. Clarify your understanding of the other's position.

4 Work out a practical agreement/compromise.

Try to work out what is at stake. Decide whether or not to take (or sanction) a risk. This will depend on:

- how likely the feared outcome might be;
- how important/damaging the possible outcome is;
- how much the teenager has to lose.

In looking for a solution, a compromise:

- bear in mind that risk-taking is an important (if worrying) feature of adolescent development;
- ensure that you and your teenager are well informed;
- discuss risk-taking with your teenager – try to agree what she can do to make the experimenting relatively safe, think about what you both can do to make it so;
- try reaching a compromise or give way on one (lesser) risk so as to obtain your teenager's agreement to forego another one.

Guideline 29: Keep an eye on things: 'supervision' is not a dirty word.

There is an abundance of evidence that good (as opposed to overpowering) parental supervision is critical for the well being of teenagers. It is known to act as a barrier to the development of delinquent tendencies, among other things. It is worth knowing about the following aspects of your teenager's life:

- *Friends.* Is he/she mixing with reasonable (so you don't like the way they dress, but that's not what I mean) as opposed to unreasonable (delinquent, drug using) youngsters?
- *Whereabouts.* You don't want to lose track of your child's comings and goings, particularly at night.
- *Attendance at school.* It is bad news when youngsters begin to play truant from school.
- *Homework.* This would be one indication of your interest in his/her progress (or lack of it) at school.
- *Health.* Watch out for any unusual changes – lassitude, depression, irritability, peculiarities over food and eating,* excessive secretiveness.
- *Enjoyment of life.* On balance, is your teenager on good terms with life, with you, with others, with him/herself?

Guideline 30: Tell yourself you're a good parent.

Let my last guideline be for your*self*. Reinforce the reinforcer. Remind yourself that despite the occasional trials and tribulations you are still there – doing your best. Don't be modest. You're a good parent.

*See my *Living with Teenagers.*

Chapter Eleven

The influence of television

It is plain, from the number of times I have suggested depriving children of TV-viewing time as a sanction, that television is a powerful need in their life, and therefore a potent incentive in the disciplinary repertoire of parents. 'What is the influence of telly on children?' must be one of the questions most often put to me by parents (and, indeed, people from the various media). I only wish there were simple answers.

Its potential as a subversive force lurks in the parental consciousness along with other possible subversives – such as 'that awful boy down the road' or 'the noisy hooligans who congregate with their motor bikes in the square'; and no respectable parent would give 'house-room' to *them*. It seems somewhat odd then, that this potentially malign machine is not only a permanent resident in the house, but tends to be found (these days) in the child's own bedroom. A surprising amount of liberty is granted to something that many parents don't quite trust, and whose 'activities' tend to go unsupervised.

Let me put some questions to you:

- Would you trust your child to an unqualified teacher?
- Would you leave him/her with a complete stranger?
- Would you let your youngster mix with just *anyone*, for the sake of company and entertainment?
- Would you trust him/her to a permissive relationship with contemporary television?

The answers from most parents would be, respectively, 'No!', 'No!', 'No!' and 'Well... on the one hand probably no... but on the other hand . . .'.

Our ambivalence toward televison, the ambiguity apparent in children's *actual* access to 'adult' programmes and (in some cases) unlimited viewing, are symptomatic of our dependence on the machine. Leaving aside our personal addiction, we have acknowledged (as parents) the convenience it represents as an electronic nanny; also the entertainment it provides (leaving precious time for parents to do chores and entertain themselves).

Yet there is that worm in the apple, the niggling fear that something *that* good, can't be all that good.

The influence of television violence

A lingering concern (given great prominence in the press) is whether the violence to which children are exposed in countless images on the small screen has an effect on *their own behaviour*. Could such images encourage children to savour violence? Taking it a step further: are parents who refuse to let children watch this week's monster movie (or, for that matter, 'Tom and Jerry' or the news bulletins), naïve killjoys or sensible proponents of a policy which will reduce the child's propensity to aggression? Sadly, despite a lot of research, there is little or no clear cut evidence of an objective kind which can supply an answer to all of these questions. However, we do know that what children make of television, and how it influences them, is determined to a large extent by what their parents teach them to make of it. On balance, studies have found no indication of harmful physical effects; no evidence that television introduces a harmful amount of aggression, violence or fear into an *already normal* child or that it turns an undisturbed child into a disturbed one or a non-delinquent child into a delinquent.

What is of importance is an indication that television might worsen a psychological problem which is *already present* in the child, and even make delinquent suggestions to a youngster already on the slippery path to delinquency. A large proportion of the children who are television *addicts* are already maladjusted. It could be argued that if these children were not getting their 'dangerous' ideas from television, they would be getting them from films, comics and magazines, not to mention their parents (not that *that* is an argument for unlimited viewing for children).

Television can be a positive influence: it may (in moderation) give brighter children a faster start in their pre-school years and make the dull children a little more knowledgeable about the world. But where television-viewing is virtually unrestricted there is little time for reading, imaginative or realistic play, for making things or talking to parents.

It should be said that the question that chiefly concerns parents – what *are* the effects of TV violence? – is not settled in any precise sense. At the moment, experts are not very helpful, since they tend to disagree among themselves, or to hedge their conclusions around with so many qualifications that parents don't know how to apply them to their individual child. (Not all violent programmes have the same effect: the nature of the violence being protrayed, the type of child doing the observing, and whether short-term or long-term effects are being studied – all these are important in trying to reach any conclusion.) Nevertheless, this area is perhaps the only one in which the influence of mass media has been studied with rigour and in depth. What can be gleaned from the complex research literature? Young children do imitate the aggressive acts of televised models as much as live models; furthermore, this effect persists over a considerable period of time and is particularly pronounced when the aggressive model is portrayed as successful. Televised violence, however, not only teaches new and unique ways of expressing aggression but also has what is called a *disinhibitory* effect on aggression in general. This means that a child who is exposed to violent models may be less inclined to halt or inhibit aggressive actions when given the opportunity. In addition, repeated exposure to violence over time can *desensitize* or dull a child to the effects of aggression and the signs of pain in others. These findings are significant in relation to the actual content of American TV programmes as shown in detailed analyses. The following themes emerge:

- Violent films can provide models for children, teaching them new and more sophisticated forms of physical and verbal aggression.
- On average, American children watch over three hours of television each day.
- Children who are rated as most aggressive by their classmates are those who view (unsupervised) the most violent TV programmes.
- Violent methods are the most popular single means employed by characters to reach desired goals.
- Socially disapproved methods are more frequently portrayed as being successful than are approved methods.

These somewhat academic findings are not very helpful to the mother whose child has begged her to let him watch a gangster film or to buy him a plastic 'death-ray gun' for Christmas. What is probably important here is a sense of proportion, rather than oversimplified either/or decisions. It isn't a case of 'any viewing' versus 'no viewing' or 'any aggression' versus 'no aggression'! What we can do is think about the meaning of play and fantasy, and the repercussions of denying a child the sort of toys and television-watching that is allowed to almost every other child. Play is many things to the child and it has many meanings.

A commonsense approach

And this is one of the first points to note about children's gun play. It isn't just about killing – fantasy killing. Most of the games of older children have some structure, and there is usually a scramble to be the 'good guy'. Many games based on TV series, involving cowboys and crooks, soldiers, or space journeys or wars, are like their scripted counterparts – simple morality plays. More often than not, the child identifies with the hero, and the villain gets his deserts (usually with melodramatic and convulsive death scenes). One researcher asks the following question: 'When the hero guns down the villain, do children really learn that "crime does not pay" or do they learn that it is *good* to kill "bad people"?' There is no simple answer; and even if there was, it need not involve either of the above alternatives.

For example, there is evidence to suggest that the ordinary child (as opposed to the already emotionally disturbed child) is perfectly capable of distinguishing reality from fantasy situations. When a boy goes 'bang bang' with his finger, or a more realistic-looking gun, he no more wishes to kill or maim the 'enemy' than his parents would *actually* enjoy seeing gouts of blood issuing from a real villain as is shown on television. The justice meted out in children's games (like that on the screen) may be rough and ready, but it can be argued that 'violent play' is by no means all negative.

One problem, of course, is where to draw the line. Do we stop aggressive physical-contact sports like rugby or football during childhood, because they may nurture aggressive feelings or inclinations in certain individuals? What about fiercely competitive schools which encourage academic self-assertion? The word 'aggression' can cover a very wide field.

The sensible parent must weigh up all considerations, as if in credit and debit columns on a 'balance sheet', when deciding whether or not to prohibit watching television thrillers or playing with guns. Will the doubtful gains for the child's personality development of an *undiscriminating* total ban outweigh the fairly certain chagrin, embarrassment and isolation that will be experienced when he or she cannot join in some of the most popular entertainments and games of middle childhood? The fact is that, when children *really* need to be aggressive, their artificial, if realistic-looking weapons seem to count for less than such natural weapons as teeth and fists.

If parents try to remember their own childhood, and the 'feel' of those childish games of violence and the film or television thrillers they enjoyed, they are likely to think their influence ephemeral and innocent of sinister implications.

Serious effects fail to show themselves in the majority of reasonably pacific, law-abiding citizens, who, as a boy or girl, enjoyed the sense of power and childish delight of identifying with a fictional hero.

Next to the influences which we definitely *know* predispose children to hostile behaviour – hostile, rejecting and punitive parents, and (in the case of teenagers) excessive alcohol, violent peers and so on – the games and entertainments of childhood seem to pale into insignificance.

What is also forgotten is parental choice. We are not passive victims of the television set. We can discriminate between the ritualized aggression of a thriller or cartoon and the lingering and crude violence of some sadistic adult programmes. It is not an either/or question of watching or not watching television. Parents can also interpret and explain programmes (especially the awful, bloody images of newsreels) which raise worried questions from their offspring. The trouble is that television is often used as a means of keeping children quiet, and their parents have no idea what they are watching.

It is salutary to remember that children who are rated as most aggressive by their classmates are those who view (unsupervised) the most violent TV programmes. In addition, it is worth recalling that adults have always made a scapegoat of each newcomer to the mass media – cheap novels, comics, radio, films and now television and video nasties – for their own failure to produce the 'perfect' youngsters of an imagined utopia.

Supervision of the quantity and quality of television viewing would seem to be the watchword for parents, especially those with young children. Children around the age of eight are especially vulnerable to the influence of television.

Epilogue

I began this book by saying that parents invest enormous amounts of emotion and energy in training their children. They hope a young adult will emerge from their devotion to love and duty – an individual with good judgement and a mature, responsible outlook.

I have indicated the influences that encourage healthy development of both a social perspective *and* an individual point of view, as well as the things that may go wrong. But it is not enough to be aware of the forces that impede the expression of the child's individuality, that thwart his/her self-actualization, thereby getting in the way of mature development.

This book has been addressed to *parents* – mothers *and* fathers – and parents are also people, individuals with needs that stretch beyond the desire to be good caregivers. To the extent that they feel frustrated and alienated – vegetating their lives away in mindless, never-ending, child-rearing routines – their personal development will be blighted. If *their* rights, their needs for self-fulfilment, are sacrificed to an entirely child-centred, and therefore child-dominated, existence, they will not be in a position to help their children learn to become unselfish, decent adults.

Appendix
Childcare and discipline questionnaire

Try to answer these questions as frankly as possible. Some of the questions are of a general nature, others refer specifically to one child. If you have more than one child, consider only your youngest.

This is not a test in the sense of there being scores to add up or right or wrong answers to particular questions. The questionnaire covers many of the issues about child-training and discipline and parental roles raised in the book. It will help you to examine critically some of your own attitudes and the amount of time and concern you demonstrate in socializing your child.

Mothers and fathers might try filling it out separately. Compare notes, but *don't* fall out over it.

	Always	Most of the time	Much of the time	Seldom	Never

1. Do you and your partner discuss disciplinary problems that arise?
2. Do you agree on the discipline of your child?
3. Do you personally play a part in disciplining your child?
4. Do you personally play a part in day-to-day childcare?
   Do you (or did you) change your baby's nappies (diapers)?
   Bath him/her?
   Feed him/her?
   Get up to see to him/her during the night?

Appendix

    Play a part in his/her toilet training?
5. Do you make reasonable demands of your child?
6. Do you set limits as to what he/she can or cannot do?
7. Do you demonstrate your affection to your child?
8. Do you hide your feelings (like anger, anxiety, resentment) from him/her?
9. Do you praise your child for his/her 'good'/'desirable' behaviour?
10. Do you thank him/her for helpful actions?
11. Do you tend to be critical?
12. Are you careful in your choice of the critical words you direct at your child?
13. Is your child clear about your expectations and rules for appropriate behaviour?
14. Do you smack your child as a form of punishment?
15. Do you nag your child?
16. Are you in control of yourself when you get angry/resentful?

Yes No

17. Do you think children are basically good?
18. Do you think children are basically naughty?
19. All babies cry. If there is nothing physically wrong with it and it cries for a long time, should you pick it up?
20. Should you punish a child of three or upwards who wets the bed?
21. Should you stop your child from coming into your bed in the middle of the night?
22. Should you intervene when your children quarrel?
23. Should children stay at the table until the meal is over?
24. Do you ignore some of your child's misbehaviour?
25. Do you discuss important family matters with your child?
26. Do your children eat at the table with the family?

27 Do you think children should be allowed to interrupt adult conversation?
28 Do you think parents should expect their children to obey immediately when they are told to be quiet or do something?
29 Should mothers expect the father to discipline the child?
30 Should fathers expect the mother to discipline the child?
31 Do you do any of the following:
  •help the child to get dressed;
  •give a meal;
  •take the child to nursery/school?
32 When you go out in the morning do you say goodbye to your child?
33 Do you kiss him/her goodbye?
34 Do you take your child out by yourself
35 Does your child take after you more or your partner?
36 Do you enjoy being a mother/father?
37 Looking back, do you think things would have worked out better for you personally if you waited longer before becoming a parent?
38 Do you think it is important for your daughter to be feminine; your son to be masculine?
39 Would you let your son play with dolls/ daughter play football?
40 (For fathers) At the child's birth were you there:
  (a) during the early stages?
  (b) up to the delivery?
  (c) at the actual delivery?
  (d) at all?
41 Can you remember and describe your feelings when you first saw the baby?
42 Could you say something about your relationship with your own:

Mother

Father

Bibliography

Ainsworth, M., Stayton, D. J. et al., (1971). 'Infant obedience and maternal behaviour: the origin of socialization reconsidered'. *Child development*, 42, 1057–69.
Ariès, P. (1973). *Centuries of childhood*. Harmondsworth: Penguin.
Arnold, L. E. (1978). *Helping parents help their children*. New York: Brunner/Mazel.
Aronfreed, J. (1968). *Conduct and conscience*. New York: Academic Press.
Bandura, A. (1977). *Social learning theory*. Englewood Cliffs, NJ: Prentice-Hall.
Barkley, R. A. (1987). *Defiant children: A clinician's manual for parent training*. London: The Guildford Press.
Baumrind, D. (1971). 'Current patterns of parental authority'. *Developmental psychology monograph*, 4, (1), part 2, 1–103.
Beech, R. (1975). *Staying together*. Chichester: John Wiley.
Bell, R., and Harper, L. (1977). *Child effects on adults*. Hillsdale, NJ: Lawrence Erlbaum.
Boulton, M. G. (1983). *On being a mother*. London: Tavistock
Brown, R. (Ed.) (1976). *Children and television*. London: Collier-Macmillan.
Bruner, J., et al., (eds) (1976). *Play: its role in development and evolution*. New York: Basic Books.
Bruner, J. S. (1983). *Child's talk*. New York: Norton.
Cicirell, V. G. (1983). 'Siblings helping siblings'. In V. L. Allen (ed.), *Inter-age interaction in children*. New York: Academic Press.
Coopersmith, S. (1967). *The antecedents of self-esteem*. London: W. H. Freeman.
Cullingford, C. (1984). *Children and television*. Aldershot: Gower.
Dawe, H. C. (1934). 'An analysis of two hundred quarrels of preschool children'. *Child development*, 5, (2), 139–57.

Dreikurs, R. (1977). *Happy children: A challenge to parents.* London: Fontana.

Dunn, J. (1984). *Sisters and brothers.* London: Fontana.

Dunn, J. (1988). *The beginnings of social understanding.* Oxford: Basil Blackwell.

Eron, L. D., and Huesmann, L. R. (1984). 'The control of aggressive behaviour by changes in attitudes, values, and the conditions of learning'. In R.J. Blanchard and D. C. Blanchard (eds), *Advances in the study of aggression*, vol. 1. New York: Academic Press.

Fromme, A. (1960). *The abc of child care.* New York: Pocket Books.

Ginnott, H. (1969). *Between parent and child.* London: Staples Press.

Goodenough, F. L. (1931). *Anger in young children.* Institute of Child Welfare Monograph Series, no. 9. Minneapolis: University of Minnesota Press.

Greenfield, P. M. (1984). *Mind and media.* Aylesbury: Fontana.

Griffin, M. (1979). 'Tantrums and disobedience'. In M. Griffin and A. Hudson (eds), *Children's problems: A guide for parents.* Melbourne: Circus Books.

Grusec, J. E. (1982). 'The socialization of altruism'. In N. Eisenberg (ed.), *The development of prosocial behaviour.* New York: Academic Press.

Herbert, M. (1985). *Caring for your children: A practical guide.* Oxford: Basil Blackwell.

Herbert, M. (1987). *Living with teenagers.* Oxford: Basil Blackwell.

Herbert, M. (1987). *Conduct disorders of childhood and adolescence: A social learning perspective.* Chichester: John Wiley.

Herbert, M. (1987). *Behavioural treatment of children with problems: A practice manual.* 2nd edn. London: Academic Press.

Herbert, M. (1988). *Working with children and their families.* London: Routledge/British Psychological Society.

Hudson, A. (1987). *Personal communication.* Melbourne: Phillip Institute of Technology.

Koch, H. L. (1960). 'The relation of certain formal attributes of siblings to attitudes held toward each other and toward their parents'. *Monographs of the society for research in child development*, vol. 25, no. 4.

Lamb, M., and Sutton-Smith, B. (eds) (1982). *Sibling relationships: Their nature and significance across the lifespan.* Hillsdale, N.J.: Erlbaum.

Larsen, O. et al. (1979). 'Achieving goals through violence on

Bibliography

television. In O. Larsen (ed.), *Violence in the mass media*. London: Harper and Row.
Liddiard, M. (1928). *The mothercraft manual*. London: Churchill.
McCandless, B. R. (1969). *Children: Behaviour and development*. London: Holt, Rinehart & Winston.
Morgan, P. (1978). *Juvenile delinquency: Fact and fiction*. London: Temple Smith.
Mussen, J. P., and Eisenberg-Berg, N. (1977). *Roots of change, sharing and helping*. San Francisco: W. H. Freeman.
Newson J., and Newson, E. (1970). *Four years old in an urban community*. Harmondsworth: Penguin.
Newson, J., and Newson, E. (1976). *Seven years old in the home environment*. Harmondsworth: Penguin.
Novaco, R. H. (1975). *Anger control*. Lexington: Heath.
Open University Course Organisers (1982). *Parents and teenagers*. London: Harper and Row.
Patterson, G. (1982) *Coercive family process*. Eugene, Oregon: Castalia.
Premack, D. (1965). 'Reinforcement theory'. In D. Levine (ed.), *Nebraska symposium on motivation*. Lincoln: University of Nebraska Press.
Rotter, J. B. et al. (1972). *Applications of a social learning theory of personality*. London: Holt, Rinehart & Winston.
Rousseau, J.-J. (1762). *Emile: Or concerning education*. Book 2. New York: Dutton, 1938.
Schaffer, H. R., and Collis, G. M. (1986). 'Parental responsiveness and child behaviour'. In W. Sluckin and M. Herbert (eds), *Parental behaviour*. Oxford: Basil Blackwell.
Schneider, M., and Robin, A. L. (1973). *The turtle manual*. Technical Publications, Point of Woods Laboratory School, State University of New York at Stoney Brook.
Sears, R. R. et al. (1957). *Patterns of child rearing*. London: Harper and Row.
Spock, B. (1981). *Dr. Spock talks with mothers*. Boston: Houghton Mifflin.
Stendler, C. (1950). 'Sixty years of child training practices: Revolution in the nursery'. *Journal of paediatrics*, 36, 122–34.
Stillwell, R. *Social relationships in primary school children as seen by children, mothers, teachers*. Unpublished Ph.D.
Walters, R. H., et al. (1972). *Punishment*. Harmondsworth: Penguin.
Walvin, J. (1982). *A child's world*. Harmondsworth: Penguin Books.

Wolfenstein, M. (1951). 'The emergence of fun morality'. *Journal of Social Issues*, 7, 15–25.
Wolfenstein, M. (1953). 'Trends in infant care'. *American Journal of Orthopsychiatry*, 23, 120–30.
Wright, D. (1971). *The psychology of moral behaviour*. Harmondsworth: Penguin.

Index

adolescents 3–4, 94, 112–24
aggression 2, 5, 8, 17, 70, 71, 73, 75, 84, 86–91, 94, 95, 97–100, 102–3, 127–30 *passim*
aggressive fantasies 102, 103, 128–9
Ainsworth, Mary 19
altruism 25–6, 37, 84, 85
  see also social awareness
anger 86, 87, 89–92, 97–105
Aronfreed, J. 51
authority 27, 28–30, 35, 116

bad language 2, 48–9
Barkley, Russell 57–9
Baumrind, Diana 28, 30
bed (coming to parents') 49–50
Beech, Reg 105
behaviour
  bad behaviour 55: alternatives to 110; anticipating 53; distracting from 101; ignoring 46–50, 69–70, 96, 101; *see also* bad language, fighting and feuding, limits on behaviour, penalities
  consequences of 66–8, 69 81–3, 109–10
Boulton, Mary Georgina 23
Bruner, Jerome 26

child-centred schemes 5
commands 66

communication with children 33–5, 39
community 8
conformity 18, 29, 30
conscience 8, 20, 21, 23, 32, 44
consistency of discipline 12, 30, 51, 53–5, 74
contracts 116–22
control of children, degree of 5
co-operation with the child 2, 18–19

dangerous behaviour *see* safety
Dawe, H. C. 87
defiance 70, 71, 84, 108
'disaster areas' 63–4, 83
discipline
  age to start 10, 18
  consistency of 12, 30, 51, 53–5, 74
  persistence in 74, 111
  timing of 38, 51, 52, 64
disobedience *see* obedience
docile child 17, 29
Dreikurs, Rudolf 42, 81
Dunn, Judy 92, 93, 95, 97

egocentricity 24–5, 26, 91
emotional life of children 7
empathy 31
encouragement *see* praise and encouragement
expectations 59–60

Index

explanations *see* reasons and explanations

failure 60
   see also mistakes
family 8
family discussions 113–14, 121
fighting and feuding 86–7, 91, 94, 97
Freud, Sigmund 6
Fromme, Allan 6, 7, 78

Ginott, Haim 17
Goodenough, Florence 90
Griffin, Michael 83

happiness 17–18
house rules *see* rules
Hudson, Alan 66

inborn qualities 35, 89
incentives 43–5, 56–9, 74
   see also praise and encouragement
individuality 11, 16, 30
internalization *see* conscience

jealousy and rivalry 92–3

limits on behaviour 22–4
love 17–20 *passim*, 30, 80, 112

manners 15–16, 21, 37, 49
mistakes (child's) 13
   see also failure
moral issues 21, 31
   see also rules
motives, attribution of 11–12

nagging 64, 65, 76
negative labels 115
negotiation 122–3
   see also contracts

Newson, John and Elizabeth 89
Novaco, R. H. 103

obedience 2, 4–5, 8, 11, 14, 19, 28, 30–2 *passim*, 38–41 *passim*, 61–4, 83
over-protective parents 23

parental hostility 94
parents' behaviour, controlled by child 35–6, 61–2
parents' feelings 114–15, 131
Patterson, Gerald 102
penalties 83, 84, 119, 121
play 26
praise and encouragement 13, 25–6, 39–41, 42, 44–6, 54–7, 60, 66, 69, 71, 83, 84, 92, 98, 110–11, 112, 118, 120, 121
'Premack principle' 43–4
problem-solving
   for children 100
   for parents 107–10
pro-social behaviour *see* altruism
punishment 6, 10, 21, 28, 32, 34, 41–2, 51–5 *passim*, 60, 69, 74
   physical 76–81

quarrelling 88–9, 93, 94–6, 97, 98
   parental intervention 94–6

reasons and explanations 29–33, 35, 37, 46, 96
reinforcement 70, 110–11
   intermittent 48–50 *passim*, 60
   negative *see* punishment
   positive *see* praise and encouragement, rewards
relaxation 104–7
reparation 75

Index

reprimands 42, 75–6
requests, appropriate 15
respect 19, 21, 29, 30, 80, 104
response-cost 49, 67–8, 73–5, 82, 84
responsibility 113
rewards 59–60, 77, 83–5 *passim*, 118
   see also praise and encouragement
Robin, A. L. 99, 100
Rousseau, Jean Jacques 6
routines and habits 36–7
rules 8, 12–14, 18, 21, 31, 38, 39, 42, 43, 53, 63, 96, 112, 113, 120
   house rules 14–15, 63, 64
   moral rules 8–9, 21, 44, 116
Rutter, Michael 17

safety 8, 13–14, 22, 50, 74, 77, 81
Schneider, M. 99, 100
self-control 4–5, 7, 8, 20–2, 23, 99–101, 103
self-discipline *see* self-control
self-esteem 8, 22, 59, 115
self-expression 6
self-help for parents 103–5
shyness 23, 29, 34
skills 16
social awareness 98
   see also altruism

socialization 1, 11, 19
speech 24–5
Spock, Benjamin 79
star-chart 49, 68, 110–11
stress 13, 98–9, 105
supervision 112, 123–4

television 125–30
temper tantrums 2, 84, 89, 100, 101, 107–11
time-out 49, 69–73, 84–5, 93, 111
timing of discipline *see* discipline
toddlers 3, 14, 24, 28, 87, 89
tokens as incentives 58–9, 97
'trouble spots' questionnaire 65
turtle technique 99–100

values 5, 12, 21–3 *passim*, 29, 32, 38
violence
   portrayal of 102, 126–8, 130
   see also aggression
visits and outings 83–4

Walters, Richard 76
Wright, Derek 21

Yule, Valerie 33–4